All Our Loving

All Our Loving

Carolyn Lee Mitchell
with Michael Munn

 Robson Books

This paperback edition published in 1999 by Robson Books,
10 Blenheim Court, Brewery Road, London N7 9NT.

First published in Great Britain in 1988 by Robson Books Ltd.

Copyright © Carolyn Mitchell

British Library Cataloguing in Publication Data
A catalogue record for this title is available from the British
Library.

ISBN 1 86105 251 0

Printed in Great Britain by
St Edmundsbury Press Ltd, Bury St Edmunds, Suffolk

I would like to thank the fans who added
thoughts and ideas to help my book take shape

For my mother and the other
family members who are so far away, with love

For Peter, here is the book
I promised you about The Beatles

Foreword

I have seen each of the Beatles many times, but it was always an exciting experience. This book is written about the way I see them, the ways they've changed since I first saw them, and of course how they've changed since they first began in the music business. These are my personal impressions and also the personal comments made by other fans.

I started writing the book in 1969 when I was working in a nursing home in Golders Green where Brian Epstein's grandmother was a patient.

Contents

Preface

CAVENDISH AVENUE HAD become, by March 1969, a veritable tourist attraction as well as a regular haunt for avid Beatle fans because that's where Paul McCartney lived, and that's precisely why I was in London.

In fact, that's why I was in England, having arrived only two days earlier from the United States. I came for no other reason than to realize my dream – to see The Beatles. It was all I lived for – then. I was 22 and since I first saw The Beatles on the Ed Sullivan TV Show in 1964, they had been the most important thing in my life. Which was also true of countless thousands of other fans. And like all the others I wanted nothing more than to actually see them and get as close to them as I possibly could.

At that time, though, I had no idea just how close I would get and just how much of their lives I would actually see unfolding. It would be true to say that it wasn't perhaps the best time to see The Beatles because what I really saw in the process was their breaking up as a group and as friends. But walking towards 7 Cavendish Avenue where Paul lived was for me a most expectant and thrilling moment. The weather and the whole atmosphere of just being in England was exhilarating. It wasn't at all the rain-soaked, fog-bound country we Americans couldn't help but visualize through the fault of movies that portrayed this country as being in permanent winter weather.

I'm sure I wasn't the only Beatle fan to appear on the scene at that time. There must have been others who, like me, had come from other countries to see their idols, and indeed many of the friends that I made in Cavendish Avenue came from places such as Italy, Holland and other parts of America. And, of course, there were plenty of British fans. We all had one thing in common – we loved The Beatles. No, I don't mean we had schoolgirl crushes on them. I mean we *loved* them. I know I did. And I was no different from any other fan. That was the thing about The Beatles. They were a bunch of really personable guys who just begged to be loved. They were The Fab Four, the Moptops from Liverpool, and it would be true to say that no other pop group has ever been so readily identifiable by the names of the individual members as John, George, Paul and Ringo.

And in turn The Beatles loved their fans. They loved *us*. I saw it. I felt it. They appreciated us, even though I know at times the fans made life difficult for them. I saw all that too. But all that was still to come. My own personal and painful last (well, almost last) meeting with Paul McCartney was still a couple of years away. And so much else happened that I want to tell you about. On that first day when I walked down to Paul McCartney's house, I was dizzy with happiness that I would at last, if I was patient, see him. And the others.

That happiness was broken a week later. As I made my way to Apple headquarters on 11 March, I saw the horrible headline, 'Beatle Paul To Marry Tomorrow'.

It wasn't just the fact that he was getting married that upset all the fans. After all, he had previously been engaged to actress Jane Asher for some time and all the fans loved her. But they didn't like his final choice of bride and she didn't like us.

Despite the persistent rain the following day, we still turned out in droves to watch the wedding. Many girls wept. Not because they were moved but because they were heart-broken. And it hurt Paul, I'm sure, to see the hostility his adoring fans had towards his wife. From that time on our relationship with him would never be as happy as it had been before, especially as The Beatles were already on the slippery slope down to the break-up.

I couldn't help thinking at the time, as I watched Paul and his bride Linda arrive back at their house after the wedding, that the depressing weather was some kind of omen. My thoughts were reinforced that evening when George Harrison and his wife Pattie were charged with a drugs offence – an offence of which I am sure he was entirely innocent. The omens *were* bad. It was all falling apart. And I watched it happen, not from the inside, and not entirely from the outside. I saw it as only a Beatle fan could – now maybe you will too. It doesn't take much. All you need is love.

*

The hysterical fans – everyone remembers them as much as they do The Beatles. Hordes of screaming girls who, if you believed the hype, thought of nothing else but of ripping their idols limb from limb. Mindless, doped-up, sex-crazed groupies who should have been kept indoors instead of being allowed to run riot at the very mention of The Beatles.

Yes, just about everyone has had their say about how it was with The Beatles and their fans – the press, TV, movies, authors, psychologists and mums and dads who forgot they screamed at Frank Sinatra. When it comes down to it, the picture they've painted is one of incomprehensible mass hysteria that put the fear of God and a good deal of wind up four musicians who apparently couldn't manage to make a loud enough noise on stage to drown out the constant screaming.

One newspaper described a Beatles concert at the Luton Odeon back in 1962 as being 'like a grinding rhythmical furore compounded of four incomprehensible voices drowned by their own self-inflicted 240-volt amplification. And if the crushing cacophony was not strong enough, you had the whistling banshees of a 2,000 strong audience like a screaming power from twelve o'clock high.'

So there you have it – mindless music and mindless fans. But that's not the way it was at all, not for The Beatles, nor for the fans, and certainly not for me.

When I came to London in 1969 it was for one reason – to try and get as close as possible to The Beatles. You see, I, and thousands like me, really cared about them – I mean *really* cared – not just as pop stars but as people. I know few people ever really understood that. Perhaps they still don't. I think a lot more certainly did when John Lennon died. Suddenly there was mourning where before there had been only ridicule.

I don't set myself apart from any of the other Beatle fans. We all cared about The Beatles and I know that by and large The Beatles cared about us. Oh, there were the mischievous fans who liked to play pranks, particularly on Paul it seems, but when I first arrived in Cavendish Avenue it was like belonging to a small community. Often there would be up to around 20 girls congregating outside Paul's house most days, along with a smattering of tourists. Most of us didn't want to do any harm. We only wanted to be near The Beatles but, unfortunately, it was never that easy.

Some people, particularly Paul's neighbours, seemed to think we were doing something terrible and often the police were called in to move us along. But we just loved them so much we only wanted to be as close to them as possible, and the only way for us to do that was to watch for them coming and going from their homes, or from the EMI studios in Abbey Road or from their Apple offices.

By the time I came on the scene, relatively late really, all the mass hysteria so totally associated with Beatlemania had died down because by then there were no more concerts being performed. We'll get to the concerts later with a little help from my friends who went to them, but I have to say that even in 1969 there *were* a few 'mindless' fans who continued to give us all a bad reputation because they seemed intent on causing trouble for The Beatles – and I suppose when it came down to it those were the fans who didn't really love The Beatles. But they were in the minority.

At first the pranks were harmless really, like the time one girl painted an artificial keyhole on Paul's gate. When he came home in the dark he fumbled around trying to unlock the gate thinking for a moment that the painted masterpiece was the real lock.

However, a real rift in the ranks split us when some irresponsible girls managed to get beyond the gates and set light to a newspaper that was stuck in Paul's letterbox. That single incident was enough to break us into two factions – quite literally 'the troubles' and 'the goodies'.

Further incidents only served to increase Paul's intolerance towards us. He once tied some rope to the inside of his gate in an effort to keep the fans out. Within a short space of time some of 'the troubles' had come up with a saw from some-where and cut through the rope. Worse still, while most of us were content to stand in the street and watch and wait, some of 'the troubles' would climb on to his roof and peep at him through his bathroom window. (Shades of *She Came In Through The Bathroom Window*!)

Those of us who really cared didn't set out to cause trouble.

I suppose we often found ourselves in trouble, but we didn't intend to. The thing was, we had a definite do-or-die approach to the whole thing and didn't let anything stop us – not the police, and certainly not the grumpy old lady who lived close by. She'd come out in her nightgown, waving her stick at us and threatening all sorts of retribution for our disorder.

One night just as Paul was arriving home, she came running out and put herself between us and Paul.

'Stop!' she cried, raising her stick in some peculiar effort to hold back the stampede. Indeed, she might just as well have tried stopping a herd of charging buffalo. It's a wonder she wasn't trampled over as we rushed by either side of her, just in time to see Paul going in through the gate. She should have known better!

Paul himself used to complain about our being outside his house all the time, but I'm not convinced he didn't really enjoy the whole scene. He would have been terribly disappointed if we'd ever stopped wanting to see him. One friend of mine who had been Beatlewatching far longer than I said that Paul actually encouraged his fans to hang around at one time, whereas John Lennon didn't. In fact, she says, fans were usually too frightened to approach John because they were never really sure what kind of reception they would get from him.

Of course, I loved *all* The Beatles and I would go to the others' houses or down to Apple or to the studios to watch for them. One group of girls did nothing but hang around Apple all the time and became known as 'The Apple Scruffs'. George Harrison even wrote a song about them. But for the most part I could be found down Cavendish Avenue because out of all the Beatles' homes, Paul's was the easiest to get to being situated in the centre of London. And I would have to admit that Paul was my favourite. All the fans had their own special favourite Beatle.

I know that because of us life in Cavendish Avenue for Paul and the other residents wasn't always easy. But I think we also brought some amusement to the neighbourhood for those who liked to look on the bright side of life. We certainly helped to keep the spirit of the Pony Express alive down

Cavendish when a man from the GPO turned up one day with a telegram for Paul. Getting the mail through to a Beatle, especially Paul, wasn't too unlike the days of the Pony Express rider when the mailman had to face 'Injuns', hell and high water. Only down Cavendish it was girls, gates and high walls.

The problem for the telegram man was that Paul left his intercom switched off because otherwise the girls would be forever buzzing through to him, and of course the big black gates were locked. It must also have been a daunting experience for him with so many girls echoing, 'Oh, *please* Mr Postman.'

'Go away!'

Becoming increasingly flustered and bad tempered, the telegram man decided the only way to get the mail through was to scale the gates. He wasn't exactly an Edmund Hillary and the gates shook, rattled and rolled as he struggled to the top where he hung on for grim death. We of course thought it hilarious and the commotion was enough to bring Paul running barefooted from the house to investigate.

As soon as the GPO man saw Paul he put on his best manner, all the time wobbling and looking as though he'd come tumbling from his perch at any moment.

'Good day sir, telegram for Mr McCartney, sir.'

Mr McCartney reached up, grabbed the telegram and turned on his bare heel and retreated back into his house, leaving the poor mailman looking helpless and unstable atop the gates.

It was down Cavendish Avenue that I made some of the best friends I'll ever have. Collectively and individually we actually saw the whole phenomenon that was The Beatles happen, from the heady, wild days of the concert tours to the awful days of the break-up. Historians have had their say. This is our turn, because no one else ever saw them quite as we did, because no one else ever really loved The Beatles more than we did.

After all, when The Beatles broke up, it was we, the fans, who were left high and dry. For us it was like a bereavement in the family, because we did belong to one big family. It may sound trite, but it's true to say that many of us have never quite got over the heart-break. It was the end of our world. The Beatles were what we lived for. Of course, everything changes – even The Beatles – even the fans. But the memories are real. And that's what this is all about. Memories of The Beatles – mine and others' who went Beatlewatching.

CHAPTER ONE

When We Was Fab (And It Was All Too Much)

WHERE TO BEGIN? At the beginning, of course. But for The Beatles there seemed to be so many beginnings. First they were The Quarrymen. Then Johnny And The Moondogs. Then The Silver Beatles. Then. . . ! But most of you know all about that. It's all history now. No, what I want to tell you is what we saw and how we felt about The Beatles. And how they felt about us. And other things.

So, then, the beginning must be October 1963. Why? Because, I suppose, Brian Epstein said that was when Beatlemania began, although at the time nobody knew quite what was happening. It was all a bit like a volcano that rumbled merrily for a time before blowing its top.

The first little rumble we can put a name to was little Raymond Jones, a boy from Liverpool who on 28 October 1961 walked into Brian Epstein's record shop and said, 'Have you got *My Bonnie* by The Beatles, please?'

'Who?' asked Epstein, having never before heard of The Beatles.

'The Beatles,' replied Raymond Jones. 'They made the record in Germany.'

Brian Epstein, always helpful and eager to please his customers, promised to investigate. Exit little Raymond Jones about whom we hear no more.

Enter two girls. The very next day in fact.

'Have you got *My Bonnie* by The Beatles?' they asked.

This was enough to take Epstein out of the shop and down to a converted wine cellar called The Cavern which was close to his shop where, he'd discovered, these mysterious Beatles were performing for a lunch-time crowd. He'd naturally thought they were Germans – they'd certainly proved immensely popular in Hamburg where they played the clubs – but they were, of course, Liverpudlians.

He found he really liked – or 'dug', as they used to say then – their music. He found it 'extraordinary . . . full of vivacity'.

It was enough to make him decide he wanted to quit his music shop and become their manager. He even managed to convince them he should be their manager, but it was a long time before he was able to prove to them he was worth a gamble. It wasn't until July 1962 that he was able to announce to them that George Martin, a producer at Parlophone Records (a subsidiary of EMI) was putting The Beatles under contract to record.

By that time the group had gathered about them an ever-increasing legion of loyal fans. They were playing gigs up and down the country and on 14 February 1962 they received their first taste of things to come when they were mobbed at the Litherland Town Hall. Pete Best, who was then their drummer, said they had feared for their lives at that concert and that their roadie, Neil Aspinall, suddenly found himself with a new job – protecting the group from the adoring fans.

But the fans who loved them were quite capable of turning on them when Epstein conceded to the demands of John, George, Paul and George Martin to fire Pete Best because, they said, he just didn't fit in. For a time the fans blamed Brian and he wasn't safe wherever he went, and even the group themselves faced hostility when Ringo Starr made his debut at the drums for them. But with his arrival, the charisma that complimented the music of Lennon and McCartney was now there, and the fans quickly forgave and forgot and accepted Ringo.

On 11 September 1962 The Beatles recorded *Love Me Do*, and from that moment on trying to plug the volcanic rumblings among the fans would have been as effective as trying to keep Elvis' pelvis from shaking.

Then on 13 October 1963 – and this is when it all really began to happen – The Beatles appeared live on the most watched British television variety show, *Sunday Night At The London Palladium*.

The fans turned out in masses, clogging the streets surrounding the Palladium and causing a virtual riot, just to see The Beatles arrive and depart. Very few of them actually saw them perform.

The very next day the newspapers reported that Beatlemania had arrived.

'Be prepared for screaming, hysteria, fainting, fits, seizures, spasmodic convulsions, even attempted suicides – all perfectly natural. It merely means these youngsters are enjoying themselves.'

That's what Ed Sullivan told his crew to expect as the CBS TV studio prepared itself for The Beatles' first American television appearance on Sullivan's top-rated show on 7 February 1964.

He was speaking from experience. He'd found himself in the middle of all the screaming, hysteria, fainting, fits and all the other side-effects of Beatlemania at Heathrow Airport the previous November when The Beatles flew in from a fabulously successful tour of Sweden. Now Sullivan was someone who knew all about fan hysteria from the time he had Elvis Presley on his show (when, incidentally, the sexiest pelvis in the world had been banned from being aired across America and only close-ups of Elvis from the waist up were permitted to be filmed). But when Sullivan saw for himself the emotional turmoil of thousands of fans swarming the airport just to catch a fleeting glimpse of The Fab Four, he was totally bewildered. He figured this had to be something unique, and so he made a point of seeing them perform for himself. It was enough to impress him to the point of inviting them on his show.

The welcome the American fans gave them when they set foot for the first time on American soil that February was enough to overwhelm The Beatles. There were scenes of such dangerous devotion that even the cynical John Lennon, when asked if they were concerned for the safety of their fans, retorted, 'Of course it worries us. It worries us to death. We love our fans, but some of them are *wild*.'

He expressed concern over two kids who sealed themselves in crates addressed to The Beatles at the Plaza Hotel in New York. They very nearly suffocated and it was only because a security cop discovered them that they lived to tell the tale of how they didn't get to meet The Beatles.

'They were almost dead when they were dragged out,' said Lennon. 'Imagine if they'd *died*.'

Imagine! No wonder the sometimes acid-tongued Beatle would much later imagine a world filled with peace and love.

Virtually barricaded within their hotel, The Beatles watched terrifying scenes as fans battled against a barrage of police as they tried to storm the building. John's wife Cynthia expressed her fears to gathered reporters.

'I'm glad *I'm* not out there. Anyone can get hurt so easily in that maelstrom. I always used to ride in the same car with the boys, but not any more.'

Despite the real danger though, to the fans it was such an exciting time, and two of them, who later became respected film-makers, typically tried to tell it as it was from their point of view in the 1978 movie *I Want To Hold Your Hand*. They were director Robert Zemickis and Universal production executive Sean Daniel, who purposely glossed over the dangerous face of Beatlemania to recreate the nostalgic madness of the day The Beatles appeared on American TV.

'We who made that film are the ones to capture what The Beatles meant to *us*,' said Sean Daniel in a report by Mike Munn at the time of the film's release. 'I'm the only one among us who was actually at the Plaza Hotel in New York. I was just a kid and I remember my 12-year-old girlfriend got her picture in *Life* magazine showing her with her arms around George Harrison's guitar.'

The film's director Robert Zemickis was just 14 at the time the film was set. He said, 'I vividly remember seeing the Ed Sullivan Show. The Beatles knocked me out.'

That's the funny thing about The Beatles' debut. Perhaps not to the same extent as when John Kennedy was assassinated, but it was something most Americans vividly remember. I certainly do. I was 17. I just sat in front of the television and screamed. It was the next best thing to seeing them in concert, and from that time on The Beatles were the most important thing in my life.

Poor Grandma Miles, who had raised my brother George, sister Gen and I on her own in the Mormon capital of Salt Lake City (my parents were divorced), must have been wondering where she went wrong as I sat on the floor, screaming at the telly and rapidly falling in love with Paul McCartney.

It was a lot more hysterical down at CBS Studio 50 where 724 seats were filled with 700 screaming, crying, yelling, fainting fans – the remaining 24 seats were, I presume, taken by the silent majority who had come to see Tessie O'Shea, Georgia Brown, Frank Gershwin and the other couple of acts that completed the programme.

When Sullivan tried to introduce The Beatles, his words were virtually drowned out by the deafening pierce of 700 Beatle fanatics who didn't stop screaming as John, George, Paul and Ringo sang *All My Loving*, *She Loves You*, *This Boy* and *I Want To Hold Your Hand*.

Before returning to Britain, The Beatles did their first live concerts in the United States, performing in New York, Washington and Florida. There were moments when it was all too much. Girls were trampled over in the frenzy. At one time 3,000 fans queued for 16 hours in the rain for tickets. Finally there was a sudden panic and more than fifty kids were shoved through a plate glass window of a store, resulting in some serious injuries.

'Let's face it,' said Ringo at the time, 'that kind of thing is unnerving.'

Unnerving it may have been for The Beatles, but somehow the fans just seemed oblivious to the danger. And, let's face it, if it wasn't for the adoration of the fans, The Beatles would have come and gone like so many of the other bands from the Sixties. But you couldn't help but love The Beatles because individually and collectively they had such wonderful personalities – and, of course, musically they led the way.

I guess nobody but we, the fans, understood that – with the exception of a few like Brian Epstein and George Martin – because when The Beatles flew back home to start work on their first film, *A Hard Day's Night*, the echelons at United Artists didn't really have a clue what Beatlemania – and The Beatles – were all about. They figured that this would be just another film starring pop stars who by tomorrow would be yesterday's news. But they didn't reckon on the talent they were dealing with, nor their personalities, nor the almost genius of the film's director, Richard Lester, who counts himself among the legion of fans and who quickly came to know what The Beatles were all about.

In an interview with Mike Munn, he said,

> *A Hard Day's Night* was supposed to be a *quickie!* We had to get it out as soon as we could because it was considered that The Beatles were just a passing fad!
>
> I think the film worked because it was never difficult for The Beatles to perform in front of the cameras. They just played themselves. What we had to do was over-develop their characters so that it would be easier for the audience to separate each of them. It seemed logical to base the film – and the second film also – around Ringo because his personality seemed to be the most developed to the public. So we made Ringo the lovable but put-upon one who was always at the back while the others were at the front singing and being kissed.
>
> Paul was the spokesman who was always being winked at by the girls. George was always mean and never paid for anything. And John was the sarcastic one.
>
> There was a scene in the film where they are interviewed by the press. There really was no script for that. I simply gave one-line questions to the people playing the reporters, and The Beatles ad-libbed their answers. I think it was John who was asked, 'How did you find America?' and he said, 'Turn left at Greenland,' and someone asked Ringo, 'Are you a mod or a rocker,' and he said, 'A mocker.'
>
> They could deal with that because they were only doing what they normally did.

In a real sense, that movie was all part of the image-building process of The Beatles. It encapsulated everything that was happening to them at that time, and as Robert Zemickis said, 'The phenomenon wasn't just records, but TV, news and magazine coverage, plus the movies they made.'

Richard Lester may have had to 'over-develop' the personalities of The Beatles, but the one thing no one could ever exaggerate for dramatic purposes was the scenes which Ed Sullivan described as being 'all perfectly normal'. The screaming, the hysteria, the fanaticism – all by now over-worked words; it's all best summed up in one word, again overworked, but which gets to the very root of what Beatle-mania was all about – love. And if you find that hard to believe or understand, just keep reading on and be patient. Obviously Lester had some understanding of it because he knew that for the final sequence in the film where The Beatles perform before an audience, there was no way you could get a paid crowd of extras to react the way real fans did. So he got the real thing.

Beatle fan Linda Tubb recalls going along to the Astoria Theatre, Finsbury Park in London, along with hundreds of other hopeful fans, on the off-chance that she might be one of the lucky ones to get in to see the free Beatle concert, filmed exclusively for *A Hard Day's Night*. But like a lot of Beatle fans, she came just too late. She said,

> I don't recall that they actually advertised for extras, but the word quickly got around that they were filming this Beatles concert for the film and anyone who turned up at the Astoria had a chance of getting in.
>
> Well, there were hundreds that turned up – so did the police, and by the time I got there the girls had already been herded in until the theatre was full. I remember seeing lots of police outside and lots of fans just hanging around. It was all very orderly by then. If you didn't get in, the next best thing was to just hang around outside because you wanted to *be* there. It was a thrill just to know that The Beatles were *in* there, playing, although I was bitterly disappointed not to have got in.

The night of the film's *première*, on 6 July 1964, was like nothing London's film industry had ever seen. Twelve thousand fans blocked Piccadilly Circus and Regent Street, virtually cutting off the London Pavilion cinema where Prin-cess Margaret and Anthony Armstrong-Jones were the guests of honour. Well, there were four other guests of honour of course, and they were the ones the fans wanted to see. The trouble was, not many of them did and so they were forever surging forward. At the door of the cinema stood United

Artists publicist Clive Sutton who told Mike Munn what it was like that night.

Policemen were losing their helmets and girls were fainting – it was bedlam. The girls at the front of the crush were held back by a police barrier. Those who broke through were quickly apprehended and passed by policemen over the heads of others and put back into the crowd.

There stood Clive Sutton, dressed in his best bib and tucker when suddenly he was grabbed by a burly policeman.

'Gotcha,' said the copper. 'Thought you'd got past me, did you?'

Before Clive could protest, he was picked up and suddenly the police were playing pass-the-publicist. Fortunately the Chief Constable recognized the figure in the dinner suit being hoisted aloft and, pointing at the policeman who held him, commanded, 'Put that man down.'

Publicity is always an important part of launching a film, and so Clive Sutton had to work closely with The Beatles. According to him, they were not all totally cooperative.

'John and George weren't really interested,' he said. 'I remember Ringo being quite good about things, but by far the best to work with was Paul. I'd have to say that I think he was probably the nicest.'

And I guess that's the overall impression everyone has of Paul. He's always had this image of being sweet and kind, and often he was, but not always, as I found out. As for John, unfortunately for him he was probably the most honest of the four. He said what he felt and didn't try to hide his feelings, which was marvellous really. Because he was so honest, a lot of people took him to be a nasty character. But he wasn't. Unpredictable, eccentric, controversial, cynical, sarcastic, but not nasty.

George was, as Richard Lester observed, at that time the moody member of the group, and this is borne out by at least one eye-witness account of a Beatles concert that you'll come across a little later. As for Ringo, well, Ringo has always been Ringo. He was the least affected by it all, whereas George and John changed a great deal over the years. And to give George his due, he has probably emerged as the most thoughtful, and kindest of them all. I can say this from personal experience because, although I can never claim to have become close friends with any of The Beatles, I did see enough to form my own opinions of what they were like, and my own determination – to break through the usual limitations of hero-worship and get as close as perhaps any fan ever possibly could to them – did allow me as close a view of The Beatles as any outsider could get. Although I never did consider myself an outsider. I don't think any of us who were around at the time did. We were, as I said, a community, almost a family, and to The Beatles we must have been like distant relatives – sometimes we were welcome and sometimes they wished we'd just go home. But one thing I do know, if we'd disappeared altogether, they would have been very disappointed.

CHAPTER TWO

Twist and Shout (And Scream a Lot Too!)

IN 1964 THE BEATLES were untouchable. They were unreal almost. You heard them on record. Saw them on film. On television. Maybe in concert. Maybe.

It was only after they stopped touring that it became possible to see The Beatles close up, to meet them and talk to them. For the most ardent Beatlewatchers getting into a two-way communication with a Beatle was not pie-in-the-sky. But during those touring years, you only ever saw them from afar – at airports, hotels, concerts. It's no wonder girls screamed their names, drowning out the music they loved, because for most fans going to a concert was not so much a case of going to hear the songs – you heard very little music anyway above the din – but to get as close as they could to the four boys they loved.

Everyone has had their say about Beatlemania. Except the fans. All that incoherent mass-induced hysteria seemed to have so many causes, according to the experts. But it's all claptrap. For the fans the whole experience was a personal thing – like trying to have a personal relationship with an unreachable, untouchable person. The different girls I've met and spoken to who went to the concerts may have all explained it in their own individual ways, but what it all boils down to is that one overworked word again – love.

Linda Tubb, who at the age of 14 had hoped to be a part of the Beatles concert filmed for *A Hard Day's Night*, saw them for the first time in concert at the Prince of Wales Theatre in London on 31 May 1964. She said,

It was so long ago now but I remember I couldn't hear a bloody thing. But you didn't care that you couldn't hear a word. You just wanted to *be* there, just to see them.

My older brother went with me and he was embarrassed because I passed out. It was just that before I went I suppose I got so worked up about going that when I got there I couldn't help but let it all out by screaming. I mean, that's what everybody did, didn't they? I screamed and screamed and screamed and suddenly my head started to spin and I just collapsed.

People helped me get out into the foyer and I remember seeing all these other girls laid out on the floor. And there were St John's Ambulance people seeing to them. The thing was, I suppose, you just got so hysterical, you reached fever pitch. One girl was carted off to hospital suffering from a fit of hysterics.

I was carried out near the end so I missed the bit where The Beatles sang *She Loves You* and the fans all started throwing jelly babies and other sweets onto the stage. My dad took me home in the car and I felt so embarrassed to have passed out like that, and my brother said 'Never again.'

The thing was, you really did love The Beatles. I mean, we *loved* them. It didn't matter if you couldn't hear the music because that became secondary. You screamed because you were excited and in some way you wanted John or Paul or whichever was your favourite to notice *you*. So you tried to scream louder than everybody else, yelling out their names and, of course, all those girls screaming different names just made an ear-piercing wail.

And I'm sure when the girls were fainting it was to get attention – not from the St John's Ambulance Brigade. You somehow thought that maybe The Beatles might actually come back and see if you were okay. Which of course was ridiculous because they would have been mobbed. But I suppose even I thought, well, maybe Paul will come and check me out, make sure I'm okay, and you waited for them to come. But of course they never did. Not because they didn't care. They just couldn't without being attacked. It all seems so silly now and I'm embarrassed to think about it, but no pop group before or since has ever really managed to capture so much excitement – just by being there.

Now I have to admit shamefully that I never did see The Beatles live at a concert. I don't know why but they never did play in Salt Lake City. Most of today's music stars play there, but The Beatles never did. The nearest they came was Nevada, several hundred miles away, but I wasn't the kind of girl to go off on my own away from home. Of course, I regret not having made the effort at the time and I suppose my failure to find the courage to leave my safe, Mormon home before the concert tours stopped only spurred me on to do everything I could to make it to London eventually.

Fortunately, many of the friends that I made down Cavendish Avenue did go to the concerts, and by and large it is their own accounts of the concerts that I am drawing upon. You see, when it comes right down to it, no matter what the critics or anybody else in the music business might have thought, The Beatles came to please, please, please the fans. And they did.

This is how my fellow-American friend, Diane, described her first time at a Beatle concert.

What can I say? I was in shock when I first saw them. My eyes were glued to them the whole time – mainly to Paul. I was there with a friend called Terri and there was this other girl that Terri knew. Terri was absolutely flipped out on George and this other girl said to her, 'Come on, Terri, let's go.'

Terri just got up and ran off towards the stage. She leaped over the barriers and jumped up on the stage and got hold of George. Everyone was really freaking out and other girls started running up on to the stage but got caught by the cops. But there was Terri hanging on for all she was worth to George who was trying to carry on playing his guitar. Then the cops got to her and took her away.

I went back to see them perform the next night but this time my seat was right up high at the back – the first night we'd been in the second row. But it was still great seeing them live, but after I felt down and out and, I don't know, I cried because I knew I wouldn't be seeing them again for some time.

I suppose most people who were around at that time re-member the furore created by the first major American concert tour which began in August 1964. There had in fact, just prior to that, been a chaotic tour of Australia which began with a welcome from an estimated 100,000 fans at Adelaide Airport on 12 June – and the entire population of Adelaide was then 382,500! Girls were trampled underfoot and even the highly-trained police horses kicked out in fright. One hysterical girl was held down by police as she cried over and over, 'Beatles, Beatles, they're here, Beatles.'

An ambulance officer rushed to the side of a girl who had her tear-stained face buried in her hands. He asked her what was wrong.

'I'm so happy,' she cried.

When The Beatles touched down at Essedon Airport in Melbourne they were greeted by what police described as 'the worst exhibition of mass hysteria the city has ever seen.' Four hundred and fifty people were injured as soldiers and sailors were called in to try and control the 250,000 ecstatic fans. One girl screamed so much she burst a blood vessel in her throat and collapsed.

Watching scenes like this on TV news programmes was bound to give the older generation (who still forgot they screamed at Frank Sinatra!) the feeling that there was some-thing demented about these kids who freaked out in such a crazy fashion over a pop group. But what the newsreels couldn't convey, nor any newspaper story, was the personal experiences and feelings of a Beatle fan.

Another American friend, also called Dian (but without the final 'e') gave me her account of seeing The Beatles for the first time in concert when they played in New York at Forest Hill Stadium in August 1964.

We all had our favourite Beatles – mine was Paul – and like every other fan I wanted so much to meet him. That had been the biggest wish I ever had since I first heard his voice and saw his face – and I did meet him, *in person*, three years later. But in 1964 all I could hope for was to see them perform so I made sure that I went to a concert at the first opportunity, and that was at Forest Hills.

Well, when they came on stage I just couldn't believe my eyes. I mean, seeing The Beatles and especially Paul was like a dream come true. And it was just the most exciting concert I'd ever been to of anybody's.

All through the supporting acts like Jackie De Shannon everyone was yelling for The Beatles to come on and for the other acts to get off. They must have thought we were awful jeering them like that, but The Beatles were the ones we'd come to see. And the *screams* – it was terrible. When I later saw them in concert in 1966 a lot of the screaming had died down, but in 1964 it was a totally screamy atmosphere.

When they played the Las Vegas Convention Hall, all 35,000 seats were filled with almost uncontrollable fans. But it seems, from what I was told, it was the 200 policemen who were as much to blame for the commotion that ensued.

The whole centre was reverberating with screams and shrieks, and there was a rumour circulating that at least one girl had tried to climb on stage and was carried out in hysterics. Many of the girls were unashamedly crying while a lot of others were at the point of mass hysteria.

More than once The Beatles were pelted with jelly beans. One hit Ringo in the head and he just shook his head and everybody roared with laughter.

After the concert several fans made a rush to get a better glimpse of The Beatles. The police came in, treating people like criminals, forcing the crowd back and that caused a lot of casualties. I know of one girl who got jabbed in the ribs with a nightstick and nearly fainted, and I had my foot run over by a policeman's motorcycle.

One impartial observer at the Cincinnati Gardens concert said:

They might well have been doing a pantomime – the screaming was so loud for ten minutes that the Mormon Tabernacle Choir and the Marine Corps Band would have been drowned out.

The fans were in such an emotional state that they were

against anything that reminded them of logic and order. Some sobbed, clutching their hands to their mouths. Others waved their hands above their heads and screamed at the top of their lungs. Some jumped up and down on their seats.

The 115°F. temperature melted bouffant hairdos as well as inhibitions. Well-groomed girls who had hoped, without really believing, that they would attract the eye of a Beatle began to look like Brillo pads.

A priest turned around in the crowd, looked at a reporter and said with tears in his eyes, 'I don't believe it. Just look at them – at their faces.'

Of course, none of these accounts could ever really conjure up an exact vision of what it must have been like to be at a Beatle concert, but collectively, and with some still to come, I think it comes as close as any written substitute for the real thing could – and says a lot more about why it was all so hysterical than any reporter could. Which is why I've refrained from using actual newspaper accounts with the exception of the following, and I use this review of the concert at the Toronto Maple Leaf Gardens because it's very apparent that the writer was a fan – or if he (or she) wasn't, probably was after that.

Every movement, every caper, every bit of clowning raised the shriek-level to a point one didn't think possible. Paul McCartney appeared the most vigorous, but John Lennon let loose with a little jig every now and then. The announcement of each title, each quip by McCartney or Lennon, each bit of mugging, especially by Ringo Starr, set loose the squeals. For a Beatle fan, the four put on a good show. Their unabashed exuberance was appealing, and coupled with the audience reaction, one couldn't help but be moved.

By the end of 1964 a new attitude was to be found among some fans, like Linda Tubb, who went to see their fabulous Christmas show at the Hammersmith Odeon. But despite the star-studded line-up that included The Yardbirds, Elkie

Brooks and Freddy and the Dreamers, Linda didn't find it quite so fabulous.

I went with our youth club on a coach and of course at first it was all very exciting as you can imagine. But when we got there we were put right at the back. Couldn't hear, couldn't see. It was hardly worth being there. I was so disappointed and just didn't enjoy it much.

By then I was beginning to feel that it would be nice to actually hear what they were singing for once. Just hearing everyone else screaming was very boring and I just didn't feel like screaming any more.

I'm sure I was quite alone in thinking that, though, because everyone else seemed to enjoy the show and when The Beatles had finished their final number and the curtain came down, the audience was on its feet crying, 'Don't go.' But I was ready to go.

Linda was among a number of fans who felt that it was time the celebrations were over. The Beatles had proved they were more than just a passing fad and now the party was going on just a bit too long. The trouble was, the vast majority of fans at that time didn't want the rave-up to end and inevitably The Beatles, by the end of 1966, were at a stage where they wanted to leave the party altogether.

It wasn't all tours and concerts for The Beatles. But then again, there wasn't much time for relaxation either. Early in 1965 they began work on their second film, *Help!*, again directed by Richard Lester.

Every day a crowd of girls gathered outside the gates of Twickenham Studios, from early in the morning to virtually the end of the day. They were there to wave good morning to The Beatles as they arrived at nine and to bid goodbye every afternoon at five-thirty.

Among the regular gathering was my best friend Sandra, who told me how one of the main highlights of the day was lunch-time when The Beatles could be seen going to and from the studio canteen. Lunch-time was when the studio security prepared itself for the onslaught. The girls would press against the gates, gradually forcing them open and bursting through, usually into the arms of Mal Evans, The Beatles' road manager, and other guards. Then they'd carry the screaming, kicking, biting, scratching girls back outside and deposit them on the pavement.

Only one day, one got through. It was Sandra. She dodged Mal Evans, weaving through the other guards like a Dallas Cowboy.

'Come on, love, you'll make it,' she heard a familiar voice call. It was John Lennon, standing with George at the foot of the steps that led up to the canteen, egging her on. She hightailed it towards them and then out of the corner of her eye she saw Ringo coming down the steps with a glass of wine in his hand. John and George had moved off and she was quickly there at the foot of the steps, panting and puffing, holding out her autograph book and gasping, 'Sign please!'

'I might spill my wine,' he said.

Well, she wasn't about to let a little thing like a glass of wine come between her and a Beatle, so she whisked the glass out of his hand and gave him her autograph book which he duly signed. As he did, she noticed the large, plastic, rather tasteless ring on his finger which was pretty much what the film was all about (i.e., just about everybody wants this ring and they chase Ringo and the other three Beatles all over the world for it).

Then Paul came along and he happily signed her book too, which if nothing else goes to prove that The Beatles didn't shun their fans as might be believed from the miles of newsreel footage showing The Beatles eternally fleeing from their adoring fans.

Sandra wasn't the only girl to manage to break through security. There were always fans managing to sneak in one way or another. Sandra told me about two girls who managed to get inside The Beatles' dressing room and lock the door. For a while they were free to fondle clothing and other possessions but bathing in the ecstasy of all this became a real steam bath when the security men managed to flush them out by turning up the central heating to its maximum.

Filming also took place in the surrounding area. Surprisingly, there seemed little security on such days, as Sandra recalls. She was able to watch numerous exterior scenes being filmed, including a sequence that never featured in the finished film in which a crocodile tries to get inside the car carrying The Beatles!

The biggest kill-joy wasn't the security men but the truant officer who turned up one day and made all the girls go back to school. It didn't make much difference, though, because they all came back the next day.

One day there was great excitement when Ringo Starr came walking out of the studio on his own. At least, it *looked* like Ringo. The girls were disappointed to discover that this was merely Ringo's film double and it turned out that all The Beatles had doubles. The Ringo lookalike should consider himself lucky not to have been mobbed there and then before someone noticed the mistake.

In June 1965 it was announced that The Beatles were to receive the MBE. There was uproar among the uppercrust recipients of the award that some long-haired pop stars should be so honoured. Some even returned their medals in protest that these Beatles should even be considered as Members of the British Empire. You'll no doubt recall that some years later John Lennon returned his MBE as a protest against war. That outraged the former recipients even more who seemed to forget that among them were those who had previously returned *their* medals when The Beatles got theirs!

However, what mattered was that the Queen obviously had no qualms about decorating the Liverpool heroes and John, George, Paul and Ringo received their MBEs at Buckingham Palace a little later in the year, on 26 October.

During the summer of 1965 they did their first major European tour and my Italian friend, Mirella, told me about the concert she saw at the Adrian Theatre in Rome. And she wasn't slow to notice that at this time George Harrison, as I mentioned before, was looking decidedly fed up with the whole thing.

Many of the supporting groups who came on first were Italian, and all the way through their acts they tried to make themselves heard above the clamour of thousands of girls all screaming, 'We want The Beatles.' Some girls waved huge banners and posters which read, 'Beatles, we love you.' They were also waving huge pictures of The Beatles. The Italian groups, who should have been able to make an impression on their home ground, didn't stand a chance.

When The Beatles finally appeared on stage there was the most deafening noise of screaming. I was sitting near four American girls and we got together and decided to call out Paul's name in unison. It actually worked, because Paul heard us and blew us a kiss.

While they were doing *I Wanna Be Your Man*, which Ringo always sang, Paul for some reason or other was laughing so hard he had to leave the stage. George wasn't amused, though, which was obvious. When Paul came back on the microphone fell over and he carried right on laughing. Then John started laughing too but George seemed quite annoyed.

Right in the middle of the concert a boy jumped up on stage, ran up to John and stole his hat. Then the boy managed to escape back into the audience before anyone could catch him. Then a woman started throwing roses at John and he picked one up and put it on his jacket.

Paul was really good with audiences, and he tried a little Italian, saying 'The next song is . . .' whatever it was. He was rather good at things like that. John tried the same thing but his Italian wasn't very good. But the audience loved the gesture.

But George never even looked at the audience and that just annoyed us all. He just didn't seem to be enjoying himself like the other three were. At the end of the performance Paul finished by thanking the fans in Italian.

The touring continued through the year and in August they were back in America, beginning with a concert at Shea Stadium in New York. Among the 56,000 fans was my friend Diane (the one with the 'e') who, along with her friend, managed to get seats close to the front. Diane recalls that when The Beatles came on stage everyone was screaming and crying and some even seemed to be in a state of shock.

She fixed her eyes on Paul, fighting to contain the temptation to join in the general hysteria as she and her friend had decided they weren't going to scream but just enjoy the music. But she couldn't help quietly mouthing Paul's name a few times.

She remained calm as the performance began and listened as closely as she could to the songs, despite the continual screaming. The problem was, being in a situation like that it was becoming increasingly difficult for her not to get caught up in all that emotional turmoil. She was beginning to weaken and suddenly she got up out of her seat and went down to the front where police sat side by side all the way round the stage, which was also surrounded by a barricade.

Then she regained control of her emotions and just stood there, watching and listening. The Beatles began to sing *Ticket To Ride* and George happened to look down at the area where Diane was standing. His mood was much better than back in Italy and he smiled. She of course was convinced he was smiling at her. She waved. Suddenly she heard someone say to her, 'Go on, you can make it.'

And at that moment she believed she could. She shot forward, zig-zagging past the police who reached to grab her. She managed to reach the barricade but slipped. Burly, toughened New York cops pounced on her and carried her out. She kicked and struggled but she was no match for New York's finest. Unable to get back in, she climbed a high wall where other fans sat watching the concert from such a great distance that she could barely make out Paul and only just hear him singing *I'm Down*. She was pretty down too.

There was another friend of mine at that concert. She was just 15 at the time and this was her very first concert. She got it into her head that by wearing a yellow dress she might somehow catch the eye of Paul among all the thousands of fans in that vast stadium! She told me she didn't hear a word that was sung.

The screaming got so intense that Paul even became annoyed at one point and told the audience, 'Clap your hands and stop screaming.'

At the end of the concert she watched as fans surged forward, breaking through the police cordon and the barricade. One girl managed to get on the stage but again the New York Police force pounced on her and carted her off. John Lennon booed them.

Towards the end of the year The Beatles were back in Britain, continuing their exhausting schedule of concerts. On 4 December they appeared at the Newcastle City Hall where prior to the performance 7,000 fans had virtually fought to get tickets. In the bedlam and mayhem one girl nearly lost all her clothes and ended up wrapped in a blanket. One hundred and twenty fans had to be given first aid treatment and seven were hospitalized.

Another of those I met at Cavendish Avenue, Barbara, was at that concert with her friend Linda. The two of them were another of the small but growing group of fans who really wanted to enjoy the music without all the screaming. But that was easier said than done.

When Linda and I got into the City Hall we could literally feel the incredible electricity that was in the air. It was as though we were in the middle of a silent thunder storm. We found our seats in the second row from the back and tried to settle ourselves down. We were nervous, excited and happy. We felt like we'd had a drink too many.

The compère, Jerry Stevens, introduced the supporting acts which included The Moody Blues. They and the other acts were good, but the last band before The Beatles, called The Marionettes Act 1, seemed to go on and on. We thought they'd never end, but that's because we knew The Beatles were on next and everyone was getting impatient.

Compères can be very aggravating and Jerry Stevens was no exception as he happily teased the audience. Behind him they were setting up the equipment, and Mal Evans was putting up the drum kit. As he turned the bass drum it displayed the words 'The Beatles' and Jerry Stevens just couldn't make himself heard any more because of the noise that went up. I didn't scream because I'd already decided that I wouldn't scream at all but I gave a pretty big sigh anyway. I mean, it really was like a dream for me as I'd never seen The Beatles live before and I was sure I'd wake up.

Then I saw Mal Evans carry on Paul's Hofner.

I said to Linda, 'It's Paul's guitar,' like Mal had just brought on Paul himself. Then I knew I wasn't dreaming. You've got to realize I was just 14 at the time and seeing Paul's guitar in itself was just fantastic!

So, like I said, Linda and I had decided we wouldn't scream because we figured only kids scream. Then we saw John's guitar brought on and some of George's equipment and we sat there pinching each other like mad and giggling.

But when the four of them actually came on it was just the greatest feeling I'd ever had. I know it sounds daft now but at that time The Beatles were so much a part of my life – it was like seeing, I don't know, four long-lost brothers, I suppose. But they seemed so distant with all those spotlights and all those hundreds of screaming girls. It made The Beatles even more untouchable and unreachable but, oh, were they lovable!

Linda was saying to me, 'I dare you to scream. Go on, I dare you.'

'Never,' I said, and then suddenly I was screaming along with all the others. It was like I had to get rid of all the anxiety that was inside me, building up all the time. I didn't know how else to express myself. So I screamed.

The Beatles gave their very last British concert the following year on 1 May at the Empire Pool in Wembley. This was the New Musical Express Winners Concert and featured a whole array of pop talent such as The Kinks, Dave Dee Dozy Beaky Mick and Tich, Herman's Hermits, Roy Orbison, Cliff and the Shadows, The Rolling Stones, The Small Faces, The Who, Dusty Springfield, The Walker Brothers and The Yardbirds. So it was hardly a typical Beatles concert, but nevertheless Beatle fans outnumbered all the other fans.

The Beatles were flying into Heathrow especially for the concert, and that meant there was a typically rapturous welcome for them from thousands of fans, among whom was my friend Anne.

She had got up at two in the morning to drive to Heathrow, where she arrived at four. By then there were already masses of girls, some just sitting in the road at the airport, waiting for the airport to open its doors to allow the fans in. Anne says it was almost a holiday atmosphere as everyone was singing Beatle songs. Some of the fans were trying to break through the glass doors of the airport building.

When the doors were finally opened, airport officials beat a hasty retreat as the girls stampeded through. The whole time there was, as Anne put it 'an incredible atmosphere of expectancy as reports kept coming in as to how long it would be before the group arrived.'

That night at the concert, after all the other star-name acts had been on, the whole place erupted with the appearance of The Beatles.

Nobody knew then that The Beatles would never give another live concert in Britain again.

The Beatles were not treated like gods in every country they played in. Just before their very last American concert tour, they made the mistake of appearing in the Philippines in July 1966. A reception in Manila was given in their honour and hosted by President Marcos' wife, Imelda. Unfortunately, there were no Beatles at the reception and the Philippinos were outraged. They accused The Beatles of slighting their President's wife.

The trouble was, someone had goofed and had forgotten to invite The Beatles but everyone still blamed them. At the airport, as they were about to fly out, they were kicked and punched and only after they had left did the President issue a statement regretting the incident at the airport and saying that the government now recognized that there was no intention by The Beatles to slight the first lady or the government.

When asked what he thought about Manila, Paul replied, 'I wouldn't want my worst enemy to go there.'

As it was, their worst enemies turned out to be the more pious citizens of America – if you can possibly include the Ku-Klux-Klan among the pious – because when The Beatles landed in the United States for their very final concert tour anywhere (though at the time nobody knew that for sure) John came out with his controversial statement about The Beatles now being more popular than Jesus Christ. All righteous indignation broke loose at that.

The smell of burning Beatle records wafted across America as bonfires were fed with the albums that fans had once stormed record stores for. The Ku-Klux-Klan gave The Beatles a warning – get out of the country or face the consequences.

Contrary to popular belief, that was not the end of Beatlemania in America. Thousands upon thousands of loyal fans turned out to see the concerts. I suppose that was the time I should have made the effort to take my first step out of Salt Lake City, and I could kick myself for not having done so. Of course, by the time I did leave home, Beatle concerts were a thing of the past but as I've explained, in Cavendish Avenue I did collect numerous accounts of some of the concerts. What follows is how it was told to me by numerous friends who saw one part or another of that last American tour.

Cleveland Stadium, Ohio, 14 August, 1966

Everybody was so anxious waiting for The Beatles that nobody paid any attention to the supporting groups. The Ronettes were on just before The Beatles and everybody booed them.

When The Beatles came on stage everyone started screaming, and about half way through their performance people started rushing to the stage and one girl was even pulling Ringo off his stool.

The police had to tell The Beatles to get off the stage and get into their trailers, and then they told the fans that if everybody didn't shut up and go back to their seats, The Beatles wouldn't come back on stage. It was about half an hour before the show started up again. Although the whole show lasted for about three and a half hours, The Beatles performed for only half an hour in all.

Washington, DC Stadium, 15 August

It was about two weeks since John made his notorious statement that The Beatles were more popular than Christ. There were maybe three members of the Ku-Klux-Klan picketing outside the theatre, but they couldn't stop about 32,000 people from attending the concert.

It started at eight in the evening and we watched all the other acts like The Circle, Bobby Hebb and The Ronettes. The dee-jay started the audience singing 'We Love You Beatles' before they came on stage.

While Ringo was singing *I Wanna Be Your Man* some young guy suddenly jumped up on to the stage, having somehow evaded all the police and the barricades. He sort of bumped into Paul and then George but the one he really wanted to get at was John. Well, he jumped on to John's back and began beating him. Ringo stopped singing but he carried on playing the drums and Paul and George carried on playing their guitars. Of course, John had stopped playing and he managed to keep on his feet while this crazy guy, who I suppose had taken umbrage at John's comments about Christ and The Beatles, kept hitting him. When the police finally removed the attacker, John calmly signalled by nodding his head to Brian Epstein that he was all right.

FK Stadium, Philadelphia, 16 August

When The Beatles ran on stage it was breathtaking. There were so many flash cubes going off at the same time it looked like one giant flood lamp.

It was thundering and lightning during the whole concert. Each time Paul tried to introduce Ringo the thunder drowned out his voice. Paul finally got quite upset after trying about five times to introduce Ringo so he machine-gunned the sky with his guitar.

When Ringo did get the opportunity to sing, he performed *I Wanna Be Your Man* and his song got the most screams. For the rest of the time The Beatles kept remarking how quiet we all were and Paul said, 'You're just fantastic.'

The rain held off until after the performance, but just as they ran off stage the downpour started. John shook his fist at the sky as they ran off.

Shea Stadium, New York, 23 August
(This account from Diane)

I liked this concert better than the concert of the year before. It was calmer and more professional, and the songs were better.

The Beatles arrived in a Wells Fargo truck and they all wore Wells Fargo badges. Paul did most of the announcing for the numbers. John kept looking on one side and waving. A man was rushing around in a gorilla suit and everyone thought it was John. But it wasn't.

Some fans made a big English flag and Paul saluted it. The Rolling Stones were there to watch the performance.

I know it sounds silly now, but I was crying during the whole performance. I remember screaming because I wanted Paul to hear me. I screamed for no other reason. I loved Paul so much, and I even went to the airport afterwards and saw their plane leave.

There were only two more concerts to go. The whole time rumours had been flying that this was to be their very last tour, but the fans were hoping against hope that this wouldn't be. The trouble was, The Beatles had grown tired of the exhausting schedule they'd kept up for the past two or so years; of all the screaming, the hysteria, of being trapped inside their hotel rooms day after day.

But there's no denying they still loved their fans and still got a kick out of seeing them make every effort to break through security. This is what I was told by a girl who went to see their penultimate performance in Los Angeles.

There were two days to go before the concert in LA and I and three other girls decided we'd have a go at driving up to the Curzon Terrace, a huge house, where they were staying. The house was at the top of a hill and as we tried to get up that hill our car was overheating. It was a very hot day; about 100°F.

Well, the police saw our car which we just couldn't get going and they told us we had to go back down the hill to where all these other girls were. They had a go at getting our car started but it wouldn't go, so they said, 'Look, you can stay here until you get your car started but you've got to be very quiet and don't go any further.'

We said, 'Of course,' and they went away. So while we were waiting for the car to cool down we sneaked up the hill a bit and saw Paul sun-bathing in white trunks. He was so gorgeous! Then John came outside – I remember he wore a black t-shirt and black trunks. Neil Aspinall was with them. They just came out to pick something up and then disappeared into the house again.

That's when the police came back and said we'd have to push the car down the hill. So that was that for the day.

We went back the next day and this time we saw George in red trunks and there was Paul again in his white trunks. They came over to the fence and looked down at us and waved.

We were standing there waving like mad. Climbing up the side of the hill were all these girls. They got to the top and then the cops turned up and escorted them all away.

The concert was held at the Dodger Stadium on 28 August, and the other acts were people like The Ronettes and Bobby Hebb, but they didn't come off too well because all the fans were anxiously waiting for The Beatles.

Dee-jay Dave Hill, who was called 'The Hullaballooer', introduced The Beatles and as they came on one of us blew a loud horn that echoed all over the place. The Beatles looked around to see where the noise came from but there were about 50,000 fans there so they never saw us.

The songs that got the loudest reception were *If I Needed Someone* sung by George, Paul's *Yesterday* and *I Want To Be Your Man* from Ringo which really got the loudest screams of all. When they sang *Day Tripper* the fans went mad and rushed forward. I saw a couple of boys brought down by the police and thrown out.

A tent had been put up in the middle of the baseball field for The Beatles to go into when the concert finished but once they were in the fans surrounded them. So a car had to come and get them and they were driven to their dug-out dressing room, and as they went John and Ringo were waving their towels out of the car window at the fans.

It was sad the next day because The Beatles were leaving, so me and my friends went to the airport where the boys were going to fly out from a private section. Just outside the airport was an intersection of a public road and a private road, and the police came by and told us that if we stayed where we were on the public road we would be all right, and they warned us not to go on the private road and into the private section of the airport or we'd be in trouble.

Later the police came by again and told us that they'd been radioed that The Beatles would be coming by in two black limousines. Well, we waited and a bus-load of people who were involved with the concert came by and they all waved at us. About half an hour later we saw the two cars approaching, but what we didn't pay any attention to was a white Dodger's van that preceded the cars and headed on down the private road.

The black limousines went by and we could make out Mal Evans and Joan Baez in them, but no Beatles.

Then we realized they were in the white van but by then they were already at the terminal on private property. We were really depressed to have missed them. We never saw them again.

They had reason to be depressed. As every Beatle fan did. That day, 28 August 1966, The Beatles played their very last concert at San Francisco's Candlestick Park. And then it was over. There were to be no more concert tours.

CHAPTER THREE

Band on the Run (But the Fans Keep Catching Up!)

THEY ALL SAID it was the end of Beatlemania. That is, all but The Beatles and the fans. What had come to an end was all the hysteria associated with Beatlemania because there would be no further opportunities for the fans to nearly kill The Beatles with so much love. After all, the hysteria was simply one aspect – an occupational hazard almost – of Beatlemania. But intent on trying to prove it had all come to an end, ITN prepared a special feature for a TV news item and managed to collar Ringo Starr for a statement on the steps of EMI in December 1966.

When asked why The Beatles wouldn't be touring in the future, Ringo replied, 'We can't do a tour like before because it would be soft us going on stage, the four of us, and trying to do the records we've made with orchestras and bands. We'd have to have a whole line of men behind us if we were to perform.'

Then they collared John who said, 'We'll carry on writing music for ever, whatever else we're doing, because you can't just stop. You find yourself doing it whether you want to or not.'

The Beatles were being partly honest about their reasons for ending the concert tours – albums like *Revolver* had incorporated more complicated orchestral pieces – but they were also being untypically diplomatic, possibly because they didn't want to slight their fans.

Derek Taylor told Mike Munn,

The Beatles hated all the screaming and the riots and the mobs of fans who tried to kill them – and they *would* have killed them. It was terrifying. You can't imagine.

If you were able to look at it from the side, from someone else's standpoint, it all looked amusing and fun. But when you are face to face with it like this [he placed his hand right in front of his face] it isn't amusing. It's the scariest thing in the world. That's why The Beatles stopped touring. They just couldn't cope with it any more. They didn't want it. After all, The Beatles never wanted to be *that* famous. Oh yes, they wanted to be famous, but not that famous.

George Harrison has said, 'Although we only toured for about two years, it seemed like a lifetime.'

For George the end of touring meant being able to simply stay at home in Surrey 'in the dope-smokers' belt'. He would wander between his house, John's house and Ringo's, sitting in gardens and looking at trees. He said that the year after they stopped touring 'took about 50 years to complete'.

Sometime in 1966 Sandra went looking for the new house Paul McCartney was moving into.

All I knew was it was down Cavendish Avenue which was near Lord's Cricket Ground and that there was a lamp-post outside. So me and my friend walked up the street until we found the house with the lamp-post in front. There was no gate then, as there is now, because the workmen were still doing a lot of remodelling.

Well, we stood in front of the house for about ten minutes, and then a green Mini pulled up but I didn't know at first it was Paul until he got out of the car. He wore ordinary sunglasses and he had a blue suit on.

I asked him for his autograph, and as he was signing – I know this is silly – I started crying and Paul got quite worried.

'Is she going to be all right?' he asked my friend, and then he asked me if I'd like some water.

I was still sniffling and I said, 'No, I'll be okay.'

So then he asked us not to tell anyone that he was moving in as he didn't mind a few fans coming around, but not lots of people. He was good like that because he would come outside and talk to the girls for maybe half an hour. I remember one day at Apple Paul came out and talked with us for some time. It was snowing and freezing but he didn't mind.

There was, in those days, a more personal relationship between Paul and his fans than there was between the other Beatles and their fans because Paul seemed to take a real interest in each of the fans. This was very much due to his girlfriend, actress Jane Asher.

Paul and Jane met in 1963 at The Beatles concert for the BBC at the Royal Albert Hall. She was there as a teenage reporter for the *Radio Times*. She went to cover the concert and came away that night with Paul. She went to his home, and apparently they just sat and talked, and she stayed through to the next day. And the next, until the days turned into weeks, then months, then years.

Actually, they didn't live together in Paul's house. He ended up moving into her family's home. Her father was a Harley Street doctor, her mother a musical instructor and her brother Peter was half of the pop duo Peter and Gordon. Not long after, Lennon and McCartney composed *A World Without Love* for Jane's brother and his singing partner. Jane also had a sister, Claire.

The Ashers then had to contend with fans going to where they lived to keep a watchful eye on things which must have been an upheaval for the family, but Jane never complained. She seemed to understand how the fans felt about Paul because, of course, she loved him too.

Then in 1966 Paul and Jane decided to set up home together and they bought 7 Cavendish Avenue in the St John's Wood district of London. My friend Sandra, whom Paul had begged not to spread the news about his moving in, didn't have to breathe a word because whenever a Beatle did anything, word spread like wildfire, and before he knew it he and Jane had dozens of fans hanging around outside his house every day.

Jane always took great pains to keep the fans happy, and I mean *pains*! She had to put up with abuse from some girls who resented her – and that included being kicked – but she would always just turn around and be nice to them. In time most of the fans considered that she was definitely good for Paul because she encouraged him to be nice to the fans too. The trouble with Paul was, he wasn't always an angel and there were times when he would run out of the house, yelling and swearing at the fans.

If he thought this sort of abusive behaviour would convince the girls he wasn't worth waiting to see every day, he didn't reckon on a dedicated Beatlewatcher's logic, because they just considered this was his human side coming out and they simply loved him all the more for it.

He did manage to evade the fans for some periods of time because he bought a farm in 1966 near Campbeltown in Scotland. That became his private hide-away for Jane and himself – mainly away from the fans. But he also went there to hide away from the sheer business of being a hard-working musician in the crazy, frenetic business of pop music.

As Sandra said, there was some rebuilding going on at Paul's new house, and a whole new structure arose in the back garden, like a giant bubble, baffling the neighbours. Basically it was a large glass dome where Paul could retreat for solitude and where also all The Beatles could congregate in peace and harmony. No wonder, when they later took up meditation, they'd spend hours doing just that in the glass dome.

Now that they'd given up touring, there was some vacant space in their lives that needed filling. It was important for them to seek out new interests, not just as a group but individually as well.

George spent some of his time in India, having become interested in Indian culture and music when, during the making of *Help!* he one day picked up a sitar that was used in the film and began strumming on it. Already a brilliant guitarist, George took the time to learn to play the sitar and incorporate it into The Beatles' music.

As for John, it seemed he had some aspirations to become an actor. Richard Lester certainly thought John had potential and starred him in his rather bizarre 1966 anti-war picture, *How I Won The War*. Perhaps the best that could be said is that Lennon gave his best shot, but it wasn't enough to please either the critics or himself, which perhaps meant more to him.

Part of the problem was that there were aspects of film-making that went against the Lennon grain – like getting up early every morning! His fellow-star in the movie, Michael Crawford, recalls that John had to be virtually carried on to the set every morning.

Another minus was that when a Beatle isn't playing a Beatle in a movie, he shouldn't resemble one, and since this was a war movie and he was playing a soldier, he lost the battle of the short-back-and-sides to the studio barber. It was a nasty shock for everyone to see John's mop shorn so severely. The one thing it did do was allow him to wear little round glasses, as he had poor eyesight anyway, and in time little granny specs became a Lennon trademark.

In retrospect – particularly since it's Ringo who carved a celluloid niche for himself – it's ironic that Richard Lester should have told Mike Munn that he thought John would have been the one most likely to tread the boards.

I think John was potentially the best actor of the four because he was the most intelligent of the four. In fact, he's one of the most intelligent people I will ever meet.

Not that all actors have to be intelligent, but he *knew* how to act. But it didn't help that the film flopped. It was anti-war and too complex. Nowadays if you look at *avant-garde* films they seem more simple, but *How I Won The War* is still too complex.

I think the thing with John was he found the whole thing about acting silly and really wasn't interested.

John mightn't have been but Ringo obviously was. He took off to Spain to visit John on the set of *How I Won The War* and no doubt by that time was already thinking how he'd like to be a movie star. After all, in 1965, on side two of the *Help!* album, he was singing about how he was going to be a big movie star in the number *Act Naturally*. Movies had also attracted Paul but in a different vein. Going solo as a composer, he wrote the score for the Hayley Mills–Hywel Bennet film *The Family Way*.

Yes, they all had their various interests to keep them from being bored after the touring stopped and, perhaps more

important, to keep them from getting bored being just The
Beatles. But for Brian Epstein, it came harder.

He needed the concert tours, because they made *him*
needed. He looked after the boys, really cared for them and
was always there for them when they needed him. He'd
wanted them to go on touring, but they'd just had enough of
being pushed around, hustled and jostled about, living an
increasingly unbearable existence. They couldn't take any
more.

The end of touring was almost like the end of life for Brian.
He rarely saw the boys once they were back in London and he
must have wondered if they'd ever get back to being The
Beatles again.

Well, they did – in 1967 – but with a totally new concept of
music and a new image, all of which was encompassed in their
revolutionary album *Sgt Pepper's Lonely Hearts Club Band*.

Before 'Knickers' (as we called her) first saw Paul in 1967 she
always thought of him as sort of not being for real. Even when
she found his house after quite a search with her friend
Andrea, she still couldn't visualize him living there.

The two 12-year-old girls sat themselves down on a low wall
opposite Paul's house. It was winter and very cold, and
Knickers was beginning to feel quite miserable.

Suddenly the big black gates of 7 Cavendish Avenue
opened up and there was Paul McCartney. Well, to a 12-year-
old Beatle fanatic like Knickers, this was just an unbelievable
sight, especially as he didn't look anything like she'd imagined
he would. He seemed somehow shaggier and he had a
moustache, which she thought very strange.

He stood there, having one of his shouting fits and yelling at
all the girls outside his house to go away. They all fled – except
for 'Knickers' and Andrea. They were rooted to the spot,
gazing at him, hardly daring to believe he was real.

'Oh Paul, is it you?' gasped Knickers.

'Go away,' he snapped.

Knickers was in seventh heaven. 'Andrea!'

'Yes,' said Andrea, her mouth gaping open like the Mersey
Tunnel.

'I'm dreaming, Andrea. Pinch me.'

She pinched her.

'Ouch! I'm *not* dreaming.'

Today Knickers is embarrassed by this picture of her and her friend, totally entranced by this vision of Paul McCartney, oblivious to the fact that he was telling them to get lost. But at the time it was a purely magical moment. As Paul went inside his yard, slamming the gates so hard the road shook, Knickers and Andrea went off down the street, crying and laughing at the same time.

Seeing Paul for the first time with his moustached, shaggier look must have been a shock for any Beatle fan, but few knew just exactly how different they all looked until they saw the cover for *Sgt Pepper*. Gone were the almost identical moptops and smart suits. Instead they wore colourful and individual mock uniforms, and with their different hair styles they didn't seem like the same group any more.

And in a sense they weren't. Musically, they were a whole lot better and, even more than 20 years since that album came out, it's still considered by many to be the greatest pop album of all time.

But at the time there was controversy surrounding the record and the group itself. Paul McCartney admitted that during the previous year, 1966, he had taken LSD three times. Not that drugs and The Beatles were anything new. They'd been popping pills even back in their days in Hamburg, but now they came out in the open with it and shocked the establishment by placing newspaper advertisements calling for the legalization of marijuana. They claimed that everyone should smoke pot.

From that time on drugs have always got The Beatles into trouble – or they have simply got themselves into trouble. But for the most part they became the targets of the law, which was determined to make examples of the four pop stars, whether they were innocent or not, for years to come.

Obviously whatever The Beatles did had some influence over the fans who wanted to imitate them. As for myself, being brought up on Mormon standards, with total abstinence of anything remotely narcotic like tea, coffee, tobacco and alcohol, meant that I for one steered clear of drugs – which I think are terrible things anyway.

Obviously The Beatles didn't think drugs were terrible. In Derek Taylor's book *Fifty Years Adrift* George said, '[LSD] had nothing to do with getting high. It . . . cut right through the physical body, the mind, the ego . . . as though someone suddenly wipes away all you were taught. . . . You've gone so far, your thoughts have become lofty and there's no way of getting back.'

Paul justified the use of LSD by saying in 1967 that it 'opened my eyes', went on to expound on how we only ever use one-tenth of our brain and suggested that LSD could open up 'a whole new world'.

Derek Taylor told Mike Munn that he too had taken LSD – everyone involved with The Beatles had. It seemed more like a case of having to take the stuff to keep up with The Beatles. George has said that once you've taken LSD it's important that all those involved with you take it as well. John and Paul had been the first to 'drop acid'. It happened in 1966. Paul told Derek Taylor, 'We had taken this stuff, just looked into each other's eyes – like just staring and then saying, "I *know*, man." '

So once John and Paul had tried it, it seemed important that George and Ringo have a go too.

Derek Taylor said he didn't think LSD was wrong or harmful provided it was used carefully and supervised. He had first taken it unwittingly at Brian Epstein's home in 1967 when John and George put it into his tea. 'I took a double dose,' he said, 'because I drank *two* cups of tea!'

It would seem that The Beatles didn't take LSD constantly. There was little point in continuing with the drug once that 'whole new world' had already been opened up, so they used marijuana instead.

Pot wasn't new to them by this stage. They'd been introduced to it by Bob Dylan in 1964 when he met The Beatles in Manhattan and set about getting them high. Derek Taylor recalls coming into their hotel room to have his arm grabbed by Paul who told him, while pointing to the ceiling, 'It's as if we're up there, looking down on us.'

Paul credits marijuana with giving them the freedom to try something like *Sgt Pepper*. But the myths that sprang up around the album about it being totally drug induced with a number of tracks about drugs were false. The record was a pure Beatles creation that was so way-out even John had anxieties about its potential on the market. 'Will they like it?' he wondered. 'Will they buy it? I like it, we all feel it's another step up, but will it sell?'

It did. And we all loved it. And the fact that exactly 20 years after its initial release it was reissued and soared into the album charts proved that The Beatles just have to be the greatest pop group, rock band, contemporary musicians, or whatever else you want to call them, of all time. Could any of today's top-selling albums by any of today's most popular and successful bands survive a rerelease in 20 years' time? Only time will tell, but I doubt it.

Towards the end of 1967 The Beatles were thankfully less involved and less interested in drugs than they were in meditation.

Pattie, George's wife, had gone to a meeting about meditation and encouraged George to join her in giving it a try. He was already into a good deal of Eastern culture and Indian music, so meditation was for him a natural progression – far more natural, I would have thought, than taking LSD. Before long all four Beatles were meditating, often in Paul's glass dome.

Shortly before they all went off for their now legendary course in meditation in Bangor, North Wales in August 1967, a friend of mine, Shirley, met Paul McCartney for the first time and from her account I gather that Paul was somewhat more mellow than when Knickers encountered him. Of course, Paul was famous among his fans for his varying moods, but by this time he was possibly anticipating the peace to come as he definitely proved to be much calmer and more tolerant.

According to Shirley there were six of them sitting on the wall across the street from Paul's house. They'd been there for hours, having arrived at about half-past eleven that sunny morning.

Every time they heard the sound of a door banging, Christine, one of the more excitable of the bunch, jumped off the wall, expecting to see Paul. Eventually, the sound of a door banging shut was the front door of Paul's house. All six girls ran across the street as Paul got into his car.

He didn't get cross with them, he didn't tell them to go away, he just stopped and chatted with them for a time. Then he drove off in the direction of Regent's Park, probably expecting to have seen the last of the girls for that day.

But Shirley and the others all took off after him, running all the way to the park where they eventually found him. Still he didn't get mad. One of the girls asked for his autograph and he gave it to her.

Then he said, 'Look, please don't go to my house any more. And tell all the other girls to go away, okay?' He wasn't rude or loud, but he was blunt. Then he said, 'See ya,' and off he went, strolling around the park.

The girls had promised they wouldn't go back to Cavendish Avenue, but they followed him around the park for a while. And exactly a week later they were back outside his house. And they never stopped going back.

On 25 August Paul was in Bangor with the other Beatles, all expecting Brian Epstein to catch up with them. He'd shown interest in meditation but had stayed behind, saying he'd follow shortly as he had some business to take care of first. Also, he felt unwell.

So off went John, George, Paul and Ringo, thinking everything was fine, not realizing that they'd seen Brian for the last time. Two days later he was found dead.

People still tend to speculate on whether Brian committed suicide or not. Derek Taylor is quick to squash any such suggestion.

'Brian Epstein did not kill himself,' he told Mike Munn. 'It was an accidental, tragic, useless and untimely death.'

What had happened on 27 August was that family and friends were summoned by Brian's worried housekeeper who couldn't get into his room or get him to respond to her pleas. They arrived and called a doctor who arrived to discover them forcing Brian's door open. The doctor entered the room and found Brian lying lifeless on his side. Then he returned to the waiting group of friends and family, and announced that Brian Epstein was dead.

The Beatles were immediately informed by phone. The call

was taken by Paul who went running in a daze down the hallway yelling for John, George and Ringo. He was in tears when he broke the news to them. It was unexpected and devastating.

Brian had been very depressed since The Beatles stopped touring. He'd tried meditation along with the others, but it hadn't really helped him. He'd stopped going to his office regularly, unbeknown to the Beatles, and he spent much of his time in bed. He'd had a premonition that he was going to die earlier that year in the spring at Kennedy airport. He was convinced his plane was going to crash and he wrote an intended last note which he asked his associate Nat Weiss to give to The Beatles as his last wish.

The note read, 'Brown paper bags for Sergeant Pepper.'

The plane didn't crash, The Beatles didn't get the note, and when they left for Bangor they had no idea what state of mind their manager and best friend was in. If they had, they would have tried to help.

A Westminster coroner's court on 8 September said that Epstein's death was accidental. It was revealed that he was taking sleeping tablets as he suffered from perpetual insomnia. The court said that there hadn't been any one immense dose but a series of overdoses that took their toll on him.

To Beatle fans like myself, Brian Epstein was more than just the name of a man flitting about in the background. He gave to the world the four greatest entertainers who have ever lived.

He also gave a great deal of himself. It's not enough to simply say that Brian was the man who discovered The Beatles. He was a guiding light; he stood beside them, always looking out for their best interests because he truly loved them and wanted to ensure that no harm ever came to them.

When he met The Beatles they were more than just a talent he could exploit. He had found something – some people – he could call his own – they were *his* boys. He meant a lot to them and they certainly meant everything to him.

The Beatles paid their last respects and tributes to their friend and manager on 17 October at the New London Synagogue in Abbey Road, just a few yards away from the EMI studios where all The Beatles records had been made.

Other celebrities at this memorial service for the man they called 'the Prince of Pop' included Cilla Black, Lulu, Lionel Bart, dee-jay Alan Freeman, George Martin, Jonathan King and Bernard Delfont.

The Rabbi, Doctor Louis Jacalis, said of Epstein, 'Teenagers all over the world found in him a hero.'

As The Beatles left the hour-long service, they kissed Brian's weeping mother, Mrs Queenie Epstein.

From that time on, despite the change of style in music and appearance, which was only a progression anyway, The Beatles really never were the same again. In a real sense, they were lost.

A month following Brian's death, The Beatles were at work together again, making their very own film *Magical Mystery Tour*. Paul had come up with the idea of making the movie which would allow them to do pretty much what they wanted instead of being told what to do as in their previous pictures. Much has been said by critics and the rest of the media about the film which was made specifically for TV – blatant rubbish, they called it. It was the first time that The Beatles had ever been knocked so heavily and they found it hard to take.

It's time we fans had our say about the film. For us it was as lovely and as clever as anything they had ever done, and after all, it was their fans they really wanted to please. In that, they succeeded.

But it was a difficult time for The Beatles one way or another. Brian was gone, and John's film *How I Won The War* opened at the London Pavilion on 18 October to disastrous reviews. But that didn't stop the fans going to see it. It stopped everyone else though and certainly sealed John's fate as an aspiring actor. Although most probably he'd already made up his mind by then that he'd never take up acting as a profession.

Ringo, however, was already embarking on his acting career. He had a cameo part among a whole host of stars in the sexy film *Candy*. It was filmed in December in Rome with a cast which included Marlon Brando and Richard Burton, as well as a newcomer, Ewa Aulen, in the title role.

Other projects from The Beatles that year included the

establishment of Apple Corps, which was to help them manage their own partnership as well as promote newcomers in
the music business. All four of them were the presidents of the
company, and they invested $2 million in Apple's five div-
isions – records, films, retailing, publishing and electronics.
The first thing Apple did was open an Apple boutique at 94
Baker Street on 7 December. The whole building was painted
in psychedelic colours. It was very much the place to be.

But for most fans the place to be was still in Cavendish
Avenue, and that's exactly where Dian (remember Dian from
America – without the 'e'?) went when she came to London
with a friend for two weeks in November 1967, just to do a
spot of Beatlewatching. She recalls,

> I knew Paul's address in St John's Wood but always had
> trouble finding the house. On my last day in London I
> decided it would be best spent in St John's Wood. As I was
> walking away from the subway station and taking the long
> way to Paul's house, a man in a car stopped me and asked
> me if I happened to be looking for Paul McCartney.
>
> I thought I'd better play this cool and said, 'No.'
>
> The man said, 'Well, I'm a reporter and I'm waiting to
> interview Paul.'
>
> I think he wanted me to wait with him but I still played it
> cool and eventually he drove off and I don't know if he ever
> came back. I don't even know if he really was a reporter.
>
> Anyway, I continued on down the street, looking for
> Paul's house but, I dunno, I just couldn't find it. So I turned
> and walked back up the road and I was just standing around
> thinking about what I should do next when all of a sudden I
> heard something behind me.
>
> I turned and, well, there was Paul McCartney up close
> for the very first time, glaring straight at me. I was so
> shocked I just didn't know what to say. So finally I said,
> 'What are you doing here?'
>
> And he said, 'What are *you* doing here?'
>
> So I said, 'Waiting to see you, of course.' Then he just
> suddenly walked straight up to me and held out his hand for
> me to shake. He said, 'Hello.'
>
> I shook his hand and stretched up to kiss him. He smelled

so nice with the cologne he was wearing, and he looked really great in black pinstriped trousers, orange suede shoes and the multi-coloured knitted sweater he wore in *Magical Mystery Tour*. And over that he wore a navy blue GPO jacket.

If that didn't make a Beatlewatcher's holiday in London, I don't know what did. Because that's all we ever lived for – to see them. And now that there weren't any concerts to see them at, we kept watch on their homes. Which house you kept a watch on obviously depended on which Beatle was your favourite. Occasionally you got a bonus, like the time in 1968 when Sandra went down to Cavendish Avenue to do a bit of Paul-watching, and got a lot more than she bargained for.

I went on down to Paul's house, but he wasn't there. I and some other girls thought we might as well go when all of a sudden Mal Evans' car pulled up. We walked up to the car and saw that John Lennon was in it.

At first he was annoyed with us – I can't remember why, exactly; something to do with Yoko Ono – but when he got out of the car one of us made some joke and that made him laugh. He then did a sort of quick step or sexy shuffle, and then he came back over to us, bowed and said, 'Thank you.' Then he went into Paul's house.

Then a Mercedes drove up and out stepped Paul. One of the girls said, 'You've got nice eyes, Paul.'

And he fluttered them and said, 'Thank you.'

Then one of the girls made a remark about his yellow socks and his pink suit being nice. And he said, 'Do you really like them?' and this girl said that she thought the yellow socks were really great and went with the pink suit.

Paul said, 'Oh really? No one else thinks so.' Then he lifted up his trouser leg to show the girls his yellow socks. He was so funny and it was so good to see him in that mood.

Then George arrived and he beckoned to me to come over to him. He said, 'I remember you. You'd been up to my home in Surrey last Sunday. Well, see you around.'

And I said, 'More than likely.'

George went into Paul's house and then Ringo drew up

in typical good humour. He saw us all waving and he said, 'Hello and goodbye,' and he went in.

The reference to Yoko in Sandra's account may well have a lot to do with the fact that at that time Yoko was new in John's life, and a lot of the fans didn't like her. The problem was, John was still married to his college sweetheart, Cynthia. They'd married in the summer of 1962 when she discovered she was pregnant. It was John's idea to get married, insisting that his child wouldn't grow up not knowing his father as he himself had done. His own father, Alfred, had left him and his mother Julia to fend for themselves when John was still just a small boy. His father did visit John and wanted to take him to New Zealand but, although he at first wanted to go with his dad, he decided at the last minute to remain with Julia. In many ways, John's boyhood was a problematical one. He kept getting into trouble at school and proved to be a poor pupil, not because he wasn't intelligent – Richard Lester has already attested to Lennon's intelligence – but simply because of his incredible rebellious streak. He was always getting into trouble and playing horrid little pranks to annoy his teachers. One master wrote on his report card, 'Certainly on the road to failure.'

So it was only natural that John insist that the child Cynthia was to bear would not have to grow up never knowing a father. They made their vows on 23 August 1962 at the Mount Pleasant Registry Office in Liverpool, and that very evening John and the other three Beatles played a gig at the Chester River Park Ballroom. That pretty much set the pattern for their married life.

On 8 April 1963 John and Cynthia's son, John Charles Julian Lennon, was born at Sefton General Hospital, Liverpool. Even at that time The Beatles were afraid that if the fans knew that John was married it would have meant the end of the group. But, of course, such fears were unfounded.

For Cynthia, being Mrs Lennon meant being a virtual shadow, always there in the background but with little prominence. First and foremost, John was married to The Beatles, and she had to accept that, as indeed the other Beatles' wives probably did. Not that I believe John and Cynthia were an unhappy couple. But they could never escape the fact that their main reason for getting married was to ensure that Julian would be born into a family unit.

By 1968 the shape of The Beatles was changing rapidly, socially and creatively, and in the early part of that year John was often seen with Yoko Ono, a Japanese artist with an *avant-garde* taste that included making a movie featuring 360 bare bottoms!

In May Cynthia discovered that John was seeing another woman and began to think about divorce. As undesirable as divorce may be – don't forget, I understand because my parents were divorced – it would be only the most insensitive person who, in the light of Beatle history, could deny that John and Yoko were perfectly matched. For him, she was someone he could really share his interests with in a big way.

Ironically too, it was 1968, on 6 January, that John was at long last reunited with his father.

Already, John was changing from the often aggressive, cynical rock'n'roller to a more peace-loving artist. George had also changed a good deal, mainly through meditation. In February of that year all four Beatles, along with Cynthia, Patti, Jane Asher and Ringo's wife Maureen, went to India for a course in transcendental meditation at the Maharishi's Academy.

For George, especially, this was something he had to do. He had already spent ten days the previous month in Bombay working on the sound-track which he composed for the film *Wonderwall*. It was his first solo LP and consisted solely of Indian music using authentic Indian instruments. Everything about him was being influenced by Indian culture, music and beliefs.

With the death of Brian Epstein behind them, their time in India together was a joyous one. The lectures consisted of two 90-minute sessions each day, and during this period The Beatles did a lot of song-writing, had a lot of sing-alongs and jam sessions, and just enjoyed being together. However, in due course The Beatles became disenchanted with the Maharishi and so they and their wives began to drift home, except for George and Patti who stayed out the whole three-month course. They all loved meditation, but it seemed as though the Maharishi was taking them for a ride just to get everything out of them he could.

Shortly after John arrived back in England after his time in India, a friend of mine, who was very much an ardent Paul fan at that time, discovered just how friendly John had become to his fans, and she changed her allegiance from Paul to John permanently. Her story, as she told it, happened on 17 April 1968.

Me and three other girls went walking up to John's house in Weybridge. It was about twelve in the afternoon. Two of us went looking in the window and we saw John. We went running back to the other girls, and then we heard the door open. We knew John could get angry so we started running away from him, and he came running after us.

He said, 'Hello, why are you running and what can I do for you?'

We stopped and one of us said, 'Can I take a photo of you?'

John said, 'Yes, of course.' He stood there looking the wrong way from the camera because he was so short-sighted.

We asked him how he enjoyed his stay in India.

He said, 'It was fine.'

Then we asked if he would pose with us and he said he would. There was another man there, so he took photos of us girls posing with John. Then John smiled and said, 'Well, goodbye.'

There was some little boy there who'd turned up who wanted John's autograph, so we all went back up to the house. John was just getting into his car when he saw us.

He said, 'Did you leave something behind?'

We said, 'No, this boy doesn't have your autograph.'

John laughed and then he signed for the little boy. Then one of us gave him a poem which he read and said, 'Have you got another copy?' But she didn't so he said, 'I'll wait while you write it out for me.'

Finally John rolled up his windows and the little boy said,

'Look, they're automated.' That made us all laugh, John too, and then he got in the back seat of the car and started waving like mad as he was driven away.

We called, 'Peace and love, John,' and then we went and played with his son, Julian.

I suppose it would be true to say that love and peace are definitely what John and Yoko were all about. John had tried to express his outlook on life, with a little help from his friend Paul, in the song *All You Need Is Love*, which The Beatles had performed on the very first across-the-world live Satellite TV show the previous year.

It's not hard to see why John had previously been so sarcastic and so cynical about life. The Lennon wit was always a natural part of his complex make-up, but circumstances that were often tragic brought out in him a rebelliousness and an aggression that, I suppose, he tried to take out on life but in the process he was bound to take it out on others as well. To all intents he had never known a father, and his relationship with his mother was an on-off thing. She seemed unable to cope with bringing him up and left much of the rearing to John's Aunt Mimi.

The thing about Julia Lennon was, she was a rebel and she encouraged her son to be the same. He often ran away from his aunt to be with his mother even though Aunt Mimi treated him like a son and he loved her dearly.

It was Julia who taught the young Lennon to play a banjo which gave him a greater interest in learning to play the guitar. He loved rock'n'roll and was able to lose himself in the rebellious strains of rock music.

His other great interest in life was art and from the time he was a small boy he could draw well. When his Aunt Mimi threw away all his early drawings he told her that one day they would be worth a fortune. In that, he was prophetic.

Tragedy struck John's life in 1957 when he was just 16. Julia was hit by a car and killed. It is said that from that time on, John was more cruel and heartless. He just didn't seem to care any more. His rebellious streak ruled his life, overruling all the other regulations society laid down, and I think in his case it was for the good. He lived life by his own standards and in that way became strengthened for all he had to do in his later years.

It was while he was at art school that he met one of his closest friends, Stu Sutcliffe. By then he was already friends with Paul McCartney with whom he discovered a musical bond. But in Stu John found perhaps a steadier personality that in some ways gave Lennon the stability he was missing in life, except for his Aunt Mimi, who continued to raise him with all the love and dedication of a mother.

For a while John left his aunt and moved in with Stu and three other boys. It was his first taste of independence. But he quickly returned to Aunt Mimi because, or so he said, he missed her cooking!

John and Paul were already moving together musically as members of John's own band, The Quarreymen, which he'd started in 1956. George was also a member by the time John encouraged Stu, who couldn't play a note, to join them. So Stu bought a guitar and learned how to get along on it, although he never really could play it.

In 1960 the band, now called The Beatles, were engaged to play in Hamburg, and for Stu that became a turning point in his life – as short as it was. The group now consisted of John, Paul, George, Stu and Pete Best on drums.

Then Stu met and fell in love with a German girl, Astrid Kirschner. She was an artist and a photographer and her interests and intellectual group of friends became more of a lure for Stu who never was a real rock'n'roller like John. When The Beatles returned to Liverpool, Stu stayed with Astrid in Hamburg.

When they returned to Germany in 1962 they were met at the airport by Astrid in tears. She told them Stu was dead. He'd suffered a brain haemorrhage. The whole group was devastated, but John, who loved Stu the most, took it the hardest. That evening their anger at the wastefulness of it all somehow drove them to stage the wildest show they'd ever given.

But there was always much more to John than an angry rock star. John exploited his intelligence through more channels than just music. In 1964 he had his first book published, *In His Own Right*. It featured his typical wit and a selection of his own drawings. Of course, it cashed in nicely on his popularity as a Beatle, but the fact was it was highly rated by the critics, and considered to be much more than a piece of Beatles merchandise. And anyone with an ounce of Lennon's own cynicism who thought it was a flash in the pan were brought down to earth the following year when John had another book published, *A Spaniard In The Works*. He even went on to turn his book into a one-act play which was performed in 1968 at the National Theatre.

It is far too easy to credit clever people with the overworked definition 'genius', but in John's case it would be hard to argue against the use. Even his later peace campaigns with Yoko Ono displayed a certain sense of eccentricity and pure genius. It would also be true to say that it was his meeting and falling in love with Yoko that really brought John out of himself – to leave behind the angry young man and present to the world a man dedicated to peace and love.

It was in August 1968 that John gave the public their first taste of what to expect when he put on his own art show at the Robert Frazer Gallery and called it 'To Yoko From John Lennon With Love'. And to celebrate their now admitted love for each other, they released hundreds of white balloons.

But from the beginning of their relationship, they had trouble finding the peace and love they craved for. Later in 1968 they were arrested on drugs charges when police, with a huge drugs sniffer-dog, raided the London flat they were staying in and discovered narcotics. It was a shock to all the fans because The Beatles had denounced drugs a while back.

John and Yoko were taken to the police station and charged. Being an honest man, John didn't try to cover up his mistake, which had simply been to forget he still had any drugs left in the flat. When they appeared in court there were about a hundred fans outside to wish him luck. There were shouts of 'God bless you, John', 'You're a holy man, John', and 'Good luck'. He was heavily fined.

Then, little more than a week later, on 28 October, Cynthia filed a petition for divorce which became final on 8 November.

That same month John and Yoko released their *Two Virgins* album, the cover of which showed the two totally nude. This really put the cat among the pigeons as everyone thought John had finally flipped his lid. Even Paul did his best to convince John not to release the record with that cover. But John wasn't about to back down. He did what he believed to be right, and he didn't underestimate the public's hostility. No wonder in the song *The Ballad of John and Yoko* he sang, 'The way things are going, they're going to crucify me.'

With the advent of Yoko in his life, John's interest in The Beatles, though not totally lost, was side-tracked. Between the beginning of 1968 and the end of 1969 both George and Ringo walked out on the group temporarily. There were also artistic differences arising between John and Paul. Their musical tastes were going in different directions. Paul's music tended to be optimistic and jolly, while John's cynicism and controversy often shone through.

When Paul was working with John on the song *It's Getting Better All The Time* from *Sgt Pepper*, he'd be happily strumming away and singing 'You must admit it's getter better', while John would reply in song, 'Couldn't get much worse'.

Such opposing views led to an inevitable clash that culminated in the nearly disastrous recording sessions for the film *Let It Be* in which The Beatles were actually seen making an album. It profiled the problems they were all having as a group and at various times John virtually refused to have anything further to do with the whole project. Paul did his best to rally the group together but came over as pushy, leading to an on-screen clash between him and George who, after all, didn't have to be told how to play the guitar by anyone. A scene in which an actual fight ensued was cut and the recording of the album went on for ever due to increasing tension in the group and problems in the production of the record which was supposed to be the first 'live' recording of The Beatles with no crafty technical effects.

It was during their troubled times that I finally managed to get to London and fulfil my ambition of meeting The Beatles. I envy some of my friends, like Shirley and Christine, who were so fortunate to see them together as a group, even in 1968, when one summer's day they saw all four of them arrive at EMI in Abbey Road in George's white Mercedes.

Not long after that Shirley and Christine decided to go down to George's home in Esher. Unlike Paul's house, George's country home was not surrounded by an impenetrable wall with big black gates, but was easily accessible. The one drawback that tended to keep the fans away was the fact that it was a very long walk to his house from the station. So you had to be determined and prepared to see little more than the house itself if George didn't materialize.

Well, Shirley and Christine had such an attitude, and more, because not content with just waiting outside to see if George or anybody else came and went, they marched up to the front door. They were just about to ring the doorbell when the door opened and there stood George in a t-shirt, blue cords and blue, furry tapestry boots.

Another girl, Jan, had joined them and she piped up quickly, asking for his autograph.

I suppose it's only common-sense to consider that at this point someone as famous as George Harrison might well have echoed his song *Don't Bother Me* and chased them off his property or threatened to set some wild dog on them or call the police or something equally inhospitable. But George wasn't like that. Gone were the days of the concerts when he sometimes turned his back on the audience. Now he stood facing the three girls who'd taken the time and trouble to come and see him and he was only too happy to give Jan his autograph.

He signed the piece of paper she gave to him and then he popped it into her bag for her.

'Thanks for coming,' he said, 'but you really must go now. Mind the step.'

Shirley was too awed with actually coming face to face with George to take heed of his warning. She stumbled down the step, only just managing not to lose her complete dignity by landing on her backside with her legs in the air before her favourite Beatle.

George smiled and went back in. The girls were quite full of themselves, helped themselves to some apples from George's trees, and went home feeling very satisfied.

It wasn't long after that that a little drama occurred at Paul's house. As I heard the story, it was a late summer's

Sunday afternoon, and things were pretty dull in Cavendish Avenue. Nothing exciting was happening at all. There was the usual drift of a few tourists and some regular fans hanging around. One girl remarked on the monotony of the day, noting that there hadn't been a sign of Paul and she wished something would happen.

There were a few boys in a red Mini who'd been pestering the girls. When the boys finally got the message that the girls weren't interested, they drove off. Very soon afterwards four fire engines, their bells breaking the Sunday afternoon silence, came roaring down Cavendish Avenue and pulled up outside Paul's house.

Firefighters jumped over Paul's wall with a lot more dexterity than the telegram man ever did, and in seconds they were dashing about the courtyard.

The girls, who a few moments before had been so bored, flew across the road to Paul's house and saw him looking out of one of the lower windows. He looked vaguely startled.

The girls hovered at the gate, shouting, 'Paul, please, get out before you burn to death.'

Paul called down to a fireman, insisting his house wasn't on fire and that it must be someone else's house burning to the ground.

The confused, terrified and excited girls were still pleading with Paul to escape while he could. By this time Linda Eastman, a new girl in his life, had appeared at the window too.

The firefighters, satisfied Paul McCartney's house was not about to burn down around his ears, left, and Paul demanded that the girls tell him who called the fire brigade. The girls were hurt and infuriated to think that he would accuse them of being involved. After all, they'd all been scared to death that their idol really was about to go up in smoke.

Then one of the girls noticed the red Mini with the boys who had earlier been pestering them. It sped away around a corner, and when the girls informed the fire chief about the boys, he took down the licence number of the Mini to investigate further. In all probability it had been those boys who had called out the fire brigade, but to my knowledge, nothing ever came of it.

Linda Eastman had replaced Jane Asher as the girl in Paul's life, much to the distress of the fans. They never liked Linda, and she never liked them.

She had been a guest at a fancy dress party at the Royal Lancaster Hotel on 21 December 1967 to celebrate the first showing of *Magical Mystery Tour*. Paul and Jane had gone dressed as the Pearly King and Queen. John dressed as a fifties'-style teddy boy, Cynthia as an Edwardian lady, Ringo as a regency buck, his wife Maureen as an Indian squaw, George as a cavalry officer and Pattie as an eastern dancer.

Linda Eastman had come to London that month with writer J. Marks to gather material for a proposed book. Her job was to photograph The Beatles, whom she'd met before – in fact, it is said that she was at first attracted to John, but when he showed little interest in her, she turned her attention to Paul. It was a blow to her when, on 25 December, Paul and Jane got engaged.

The following May John and Paul flew to New York for a series of business meetings concerning The Beatles' company, Apple. They were accompanied by Mal Evans, publicity manager Derek Taylor and Alex Madris, an electronics wizard in Apple's employ. At a press conference held at the Americana Hotel on 13 May, Linda Eastman turned up and slipped Paul her phone number. For a few days they were in each other's company, and Paul was enchanted by Linda's four-year-old daughter, Heather.

Linda even stayed in an apartment with Paul and John following a party on their last night in New York. She saw them off at the airport as they flew back home to London, and she was left wondering about her relationship with Paul.

The next month Paul returned to the United States to announce at a Capitol Records convention in Los Angeles that in future all Beatle records would be released on the Apple label throughout the world except in America where they still had a contract with Capitol. It was also revealed that the first artist (apart from The Beatles) to be signed by Apple was a Welsh singer called Mary Hopkin. Her first record, *Those Were The Days*, was produced by Paul himself, and he also played some of the instruments on the recording which proved to be a smash hit.

While in LA Paul invited Linda to spend a week with him, but when she returned to New York and he to London, she was worried and puzzled by his lack of commitment, even though by this time his relationship with Jane Asher seemed to be quickly declining.

Just how bad things were between Jane and Paul was made public on 20 June when Jane appeared on *The Simon Dee Show* on BBC TV and announced that her engagement to Paul McCartney was off. It was a shock to the fans. Part of the problem had been that Paul had wanted her to give up her acting career and she had refused. He'd actually asked her to marry him several times before she had said yes because she was always concerned that she would end up being part of a 'gang'!

We all thought that she and Paul made a lovely couple and they appeared to be very happy and very much in love. After the split Jane said, 'I know it sounds corny, but we still see each other and love each other, but it hasn't worked out. Perhaps we will be childhood sweethearts and meet again and get married when we're about 70.'

So much was happening in the private lives of The Beatles that it was almost easy to forget that they still had work to do as a group. So on 4 September they got together at Twickenham Film Studios, along with 300 lucky fans, to make a film – they call them pop videos today – of *Hey Jude*, their new single which, I believe, boasts the longest fade-out in recording history. More important for the fans – at least, those who attended – it was a rare opportunity to spend several hours with The Beatles in seventh heaven. And if anyone should think that at that time in 1968 The Beatles were having the kind of problems that would be revealed in *Let It Be* the following year, then Sandra would definitely argue the point, as she was there and provided me with this account.

It began at Trident recording studios where Mal Evans said that something wonderful was going to happen the following Tuesday.

So I took the day off work and went down to the recording studios with my friends, and Mal told us that there were tickets to *Hey Jude*. He also said that we would be the only ones there, but as it happened this wasn't true. Mal told us to meet at Victoria Station and to dress as though for work.

On that day, we arrived at Victoria Station two hours early and went and sat in the Wimpy bar. When the coach finally arrived, I'm afraid I ran out without paying my bill because I just couldn't wait. I was nervous because I thought that there would just be me, my friends and a few others going, but the coach was packed full.

When we got to the studios we all had to queue up and there were two girls crying because they couldn't get in.

Inside, The Beatles finally arrived in the sound stage and Paul waved to everyone. All the fans were supposed to rehearse with The Beatles for about three hours. We were told that as soon as the la-la bit at the end starts, we should rush up to The Beatles and start singing. But all the rehearsals went wrong. We kept mucking it up so we could remain with The Beatles longer!

Everyone was just larking about for three hours and the total rehearsal lasted for six hours.

Paul was singing *Hey Jude* in different languages, and The Beatles sang other songs just for fun like *Little Green Apples*.

It was just fantastic – the best thing that ever happened. At the end of the recording everyone was saying that they couldn't get home, but Paul said he would hire a car for those who couldn't get home by coach.

Paul could be good like that. The next day he gave three girls a lift from Apple to EMI and he asked the girls how they enjoyed the show. He said that he'd like to do another one, but unfortunately The Beatles never did.

Meanwhile, back in America, Linda Eastman was still in suspense about Paul until November when he went to New York to bring her and Heather back to London. He also met her father, Lee, and her brother, John, who were partners in the New York law firm, Eastman and Eastman. This was something of a fateful meeting because in January 1969 an American accountant, Alan Klein, was appointed to look after the financial problems that Apple was already facing. John, George and Ringo were keen on having Klein (who'd looked after the interests of The Rolling Stones among other artists) advise them on all business matters, but Paul didn't trust him – he wanted Eastman and Eastman to take care of The Beatles' affairs.

Some say it was this disagreement between Paul and the other three Beatles that caused the eventual split. It was certainly a heavy wedge driven into the group, but there were other factors, such as the artistic differences between John and Paul. Some people blamed Yoko for the split. I don't. I blame Linda.

CHAPTER FOUR

Sun King

DOMINIQUE WAS FROM Italy. She loved George Harrison. Called him Sun King. I said to her, 'Do you remember it at all – you know – all the waiting and watching?'

She said she did.

I said, 'Tell me about it. Tell me what it was like waiting to see George. Just as you remember it.'

These are her own words.

A day in the life of a fan

I spring to my feet, picking up all my things in the dark; bottle of water, sandwiches, paper – where the hell is my doll?

'Ulixes, where are you? Oh, there you are. Come on, love, some bad people are coming.'

Is there anything else? My bag! My blanket!

I'm there all alone in the middle of the road outside the EMI studios with all my things in my arms, with the blanket under my feet as the police van stops quietly near by. I feel dead.

'What are you doing here?' they ask. 'How old are you? Do your parents know you're still out? What are all those things for? Where do you live? Where are you from? Name and address?'

I'm just standing there, hugging my doll, terrified. I don't know what to do, what to say. I feel like crying. The bottle of water slips from my hands and smashes on the pavement. Oh God, they're going to put me in jail now.

'Watch what you're doing,' they shout at me. 'Little madam!'

I feel smaller and smaller. I put all my things on the pavement and pick up all the pieces of broken glass. They're looking at me, grinning. (Go home, police, go home and have a good night's sleep. It's late.) I'm nearly crying.

'Okay, go home now,' they say. 'Where do you live?'

'Near here.'

'Then go home.'

I pick up all my things once more and slowly walk away. Just around the corner I stop and look back. The police have gone. I run back to my place outside the studios in Abbey Road and sit down again.

'It's okay, Ulixes. We didn't get arrested tonight.'

The other girls reappear, gathering around.

'Why didn't you run away as soon as we told you to?'

'I couldn't leave all my things here. Anyway they haven't been too bad.'

I feel better but thirsty and I haven't got any more water. Never mind, as long as *he's* in there, everything is okay!

At 1.30 am 'piggies' come walking down the street again, laughing at us, shouting, 'The Beatles'll never come out tonight, girls. Better go home.'

I'd like to kill them – *Hare Krishna!* I jump up and shout back, 'You'll never be a Beatle.'

They walk silently away – *bastards!*

Half an hour passes and I'm so so sleepy and so cold. One blanket just isn't enough tonight.

I pray, 'Georgie, come out. Georgie, come out please. It's late, time to go home.'

It's always the same time after 1.30. I start feeling miserable, stupid, the most miserable thing in the world. I'd like to die, and he doesn't come out, and it's so late and it's so cold. *George!*

At 2.30 a man and a woman pass by, hand in hand. They stop and look at me, freezing, nearly dead, wrapped up in my blanket.

'What are you waiting for?' he asks.

'George is in there,' I answer.

'George who?'

'What? George Harrison, of course.'

They look at each other. 'And are you staying here all night long just to see a Beatle?'

'Yes, why not?'

'And if it's raining?'

'I wait in the rain.'

'And if it's snowing?'

'I wait in the snow.'

'And do you think this is a good thing? Do you think this is love? Listen to me, girl, this is just fanaticism, not love.'

'That's right,' says the woman. 'I love my man, but I wouldn't wait for him in the rain.'

'And I love her very much,' he says, 'but I wouldn't wait for her in the snow. See?'

I look at them and see how poor they are.

'So you love each other only when the sun is shining?' I ask. They don't answer but just walk away. And I'm still so cold, so, so sleepy.

It's funny, but after three in the morning, I'm so sleepy, so cold, so miserable, that I feel happy. I start laughing for nothing, singing songs loudly, shouting *Hare Krishna* to everybody, slapping all the other girls on their shoulders. I jump around full of happiness. Funny girl!

It's 3.30 and I take my necklace in my hands and chant – *Hare Krishna Hare Krishna Krishna Krishna Hare Hare Rama Hare Rama Rama Rama Hare Hare. . . .*

Jesus said that a man makes himself what he wants to be. I'm making myself happy. *Hare Krishna Hare Krishna.*

The birds begin to sing at 5.00 am. There is a strange beautiful light in the sky. Nature is waking up. The flowers open their corollas. The petals talk to the birds. The nightingales sing to the leaves and the trees, and all together they say 'Good morning!' to me. I believe I am in love.

The sun comes up and I think, something good is going to happen.

Then suddenly I catch a glimpse of George passing through EMI reception. Here he is, Sun King, shining on me who was so tired and cold. I'm so happy to see all these little things this morning – the birds, the flowers, the trees. God, my God, you're there giving brightness to the sun, looking and smiling at me who loves you so much. I know you're there, you never leave me, always protecting me, caressing me with your hands. I feel your look giving warmth to my soul. Thank you for being in there George. If I hadn't waited for you this morning, I couldn't have seen nature waking up. I couldn't have seen my God.

It's six in the morning and Mal brings a guitar out to George's car. Perhaps he's come out now.

'Come on, Ulixes, come and see George.' I put everything back into my paper bag. I comb my hair and look at my face in my mirror. Perfect. Very pale cheeks and black rings around the eyes. Perfect.

Fifteen minutes later he is standing on the steps of EMI, talking to Klaus. I can see an aura, a white shining light around him, like an aura of petals around a flower.

He gets in his car and just before driving out of the gate he calls to Mal. They talk for a minute and then he drives through the gate. He pulls up near me and, smiling, he says to me, 'Good morning.'

I hug Ulixes more than ever. 'Good morning George.'

And then he disappears at the bottom of the road. He's going home to sleep. He must be tired. Poor darling, I hope he gets home soon.

Okay, it's over. Funny how after all those hours of waiting it all happens in just a few seconds. But that was what I'd been waiting for. It's just what I'd wanted. I didn't want nor expect anything else. Just to see with my eyes that he's all right, happy, cheerful. That was what I'd been hoping for, just that. But it's such a lot for me, oh such a lot.

After giving Mal the stamps I always save for him I walk slowly home. It takes about half an hour, but I don't care. I like walking home in the early morning with the sun shining on me, thinking about George. And I suddenly realize I actually saw *him*. He's really here, he's living, eating, drinking, smiling, walking, breathing, alive – and I don't care if he doesn't even know me, if I'm not part of his life. He's alive. It's enough to make me cry with joy, and I pray, 'Oh God, thank you for George being alive.' It's so beautiful to cry with joy.

I manage to get some sleep and to work through the day, doing my job without any interest or real attention to what I'm doing. At 6.30 I rush out, not even saying 'Goodbye' to anyone. I'm smiling, feeling happy like a child with a new toy, because this is what I've been looking forward to all day long. I'm so happy I don't even feel the crush of people on the bus pushing me like mad. I just don't care about that. I see that

Oxford Street is more crowded than usual. Next stop is Baker Street where the Apple shop was. Then I'm at St John's Wood – I'm there. I jump off the bus and run down Abbey Road to the EMI studios.

His car is parked there, next to Mal's. So George *is* recording this evening. 'Thank you my God.'

At eight in the evening I eat my sandwiches and drink a little water, my eyes constantly fixed on that bit of the reception area where I might get a glimpse of him if walks from the control room to the studio.

'How are you today?' a girl asks.

'Okay, as long as he's in there. I'm okay.'

By ten the occupants of the house opposite EMI are complaining.

'What the hell are you doing, you stupid girls, sitting there all night long, disturbing the neighbourhood?'

They just don't know, do they? They just don't understand that George is in. We tell them to go to hell.

An hour later and I start feeling cold and sleepy . . . sleepy . . . more and more sleepy. . . .

'Wake up!' cry the girls, shaking me. 'George passed through reception.'

'What was he wearing?'

'Orange shirt and jeans.'

I don't feel cold anymore. Just happy. I had seen a light around him yesterday, an inner light so strong that I really could see it. He really has got something inside himself. How can somebody think of just going to bed with him?

It's midnight and I'm cold again. I wrap myself in my blanket and feel better. But I'm so sleepy. My eyes close. 'Good night Ulixes.'

Then I remember that I must keep my eyes open. I must see when he comes out. That's why I'm here, to see him. But I don't even know that I'm falling asleep.

'Wake up! Come on, hurry up! Hide away! Police are coming!'

The cries of the other girls wake me suddenly. Here we go again. The police come and move me on. I wait until they've gone and then return to my place.

It's 7.30 by the time I get home, exhausted, falling into bed.

But I'm so tired I can't sleep. I can still see his smile, his hair, his pure shining eyes upon me as he said 'Good morning.' His eyes. Millions of eyes float before me. I feel punch-drunk. If only I could sleep for a while.

The nine o'clock alarm shrieks, 'Wake up, wash up, dress up, get out and on the bus and get to work late as usual.'

I manage to do my work, drinking three or four cups of black coffee every hour. I hardly see what I'm doing, but somehow I do it.

At lunchtime everyone goes out, leaving me to sleep with my head on my desk. Then everyone returns and I restart work, eating some sandwiches and drinking my twentieth or so cup of strong black coffee. Then at 6.30 I'm off again without saying goodbye because this is what I've been waiting for all day long. This is what I live for.

That's what she remembers, and I suppose you think, 'Silly girl, why do you do it?' But that's because you don't understand. I understand. For her as well as for me, the most important thing in our lives was The Beatles.

CHAPTER FIVE

Yesterday

I COULDN'T DENY that Paul McCartney was going to make a loving father as I watched him carrying Linda's daughter, Heather, in his arms all the way from school back to his house at number seven Cavendish Avenue. And you couldn't deny that he and Linda were very much in love. At that time I didn't know too much about Linda Eastman, and on this day, my second down Cavendish Avenue, none of the fans had any idea that a week later Paul and Linda would be man and wife.

I'd stood alone outside the huge black gates that barred every unwelcome visitor from Paul's house. I don't know where all the other girls were that day, but I was delighted and surprised to be the only one there, especially as I was seeing Paul for the very first time in the flesh.

On arriving there I'd felt a little lonely, having made some friends among the fans the previous day, and I was actually wandering off down the road away from Paul's house when I suddenly heard a voice from behind the gates.

That sounds like Donovan, the protest singer, I thought, and sure enough as the gates swung open out came Donovan followed by Paul, Linda and Paul's enormous sheepdog Martha. It seemed amazing, not just to see Paul, but to watch him going off down the street without getting into a car, as I'd expected he would do if he were to emerge.

He and the others wandered off down Cavendish Avenue and I followed at a discreet distance. They turned right and headed towards the school. When Heather came out, Paul didn't hesitate in greeting her and scooping her up in his arms. I then followed them back to his house where they all disappeared inside.

This was my first real look at Paul and I have to say he was even more handsome in person than he'd ever looked in even the most complimentary of photographs. He was clean shaven and had long hair. He was glorious and unbelievably fantastic.

I suppose the reason he and Linda had felt safe to walk to the school and back was simply because of the absence of a fan gathering. Usually there were girls bustling around outside his house as I'd discovered the previous day.

Then I had approached the house with both trepidation and exhilaration as I really had hoped to catch my first glimpse of a Beatle. I'd also felt very much like a stranger suddenly being among all those girls who had the very same purpose in mind as I did. But it only took a few days before I began to feel a part of that community, although it was disappointing not to have seen Paul that first day.

At that time I was living with a kind family in Rainham in Essex, having finally arrived in England on 4 March. It may have been the final year of the decade but even in 1969 the Sixties were still swinging. For someone like me from a Mormon home in Salt Lake, coming to London was as exciting as someone from England going to Disneyland. It was all so unbelievable. Except that unlike Disneyland, the swinging scene of London wasn't exactly the essence of innocence and childhood fantasies. Hippies were a familiar sight everywhere, tuning in, turning on and tripping out, and very definitely making love not war.

I wasn't totally unprepared for all this as I'd spent the previous six months in New York working at the Visiting Nurse Service, having finally found the courage and determination to leave home. Three months before that I had actually been on my way to England for the sole purpose of Beatlewatching. Unfortunately, that dream quickly turned to a nightmare because when I got to Customs at Heathrow Airport, I was honest and admitted that I had arrived with the intention of finding a job. At the time all I thought about was how desperate I was to meet The Beatles and I knew I had to get a job to be able to stay in London.

I was immediately deported, and as upset as I was to have been robbed of my dream, I was determined to get it back. And I did.

The day I watched Paul collect Heather from school, I also observed how considerate he could be to the public when in the mood. That afternoon he came out of his gate and stood talking to a lady and the little girl who was with her. I stood close by, resisting the temptation to simply reach out and touch him. Later he got into Donovan's car and they drove off.

There are certain frustrations to Beatlewatching – like when you can't see them properly. But I did get to see all four Beatles the day before Paul's wedding was announced. Considering this was the period when they were beginning to break up, in retrospect it was quite surprising to see all four turn up at Paul's house. First Ringo and John arrived together and it was frustrating not to see much of them but their backs as they were walking away from me. But when George arrived I saw his face – and was he gorgeous!

It was the very next day, 11 March, as I made my way down to Apple headquarters that I saw the horrible news emblazoned on an evening paper headline – Beatle Paul To Marry Tomorrow.

It hit all the fans hard. They had never liked Linda from the moment she came on to the scene. She was so different from Jane. I think Linda was a bit of a snob who thought she was better than the fans. But we had all loved Paul for a lot longer than she had. Just the thought that he was getting married at all was something I found hard to swallow, but for all the other girls, as I quickly discovered, it was the fact that he was marrying *her*.

Having seen the headline, I hurried on down to Apple to wait with all the other fans to find out if it was really true. There were newspaper photographers and reporters everywhere and pictures of the worried fans were snapped left, right and centre.

Finally Paul emerged and when asked outright if the news was true, he said, 'Yes, it's true.'

We were all devastated, but I couldn't help smiling when George appeared with a sarcastic grin and sang, 'Paul's getting married in the morning.' I really don't think he approved at all.

That night Paul wasn't at home with Linda but down at Apple recording. I mean, fancy spending the night before you get married in a recording studio! As far as I know he didn't even take the other Beatles out for a stag night. All this time Linda was alone in the house while outside we were congregating in droves. We were all very angry, to say the least, and our mood wasn't lost on her as she phoned the police for help. According to the following day's newspapers, she really had feared for her life, and so the police turned up and we all turned tail and ran for it. At least, I did. I just ran as quickly as I could away from the house because I had visions of spending the night in jail if I'd been caught.

The next day the falling rain matched the spirits of the fans as we stood outside Cavendish Avenue, weeping openly. The wedding had been delayed because Paul's best man and brother, Mike McGear (of The Scaffold) was held up on a late train.

After the wedding Paul and Linda went to a church in St John's Wood to have their marriage blessed. I remained at Cavendish Avenue to await his return, as did a host of reporters and the other fans who were still crying.

I watched as Paul and his bride pulled in through the gates. Pressed for a statement, Paul said that he would have married Linda sooner or later, but Linda had made it sooner rather than later. The fact was, she was three months pregnant.

That evening George and Pattie were arrested for possession of drugs. The day had begun badly enough, but now it was deteriorating into a black nightmare. I couldn't help feeling that the whole day was an omen – a very bad omen of things to come.

'Your baby is going to break a lot of girls' hearts with those beautiful big brown eyes and long lashes,' everyone told Jim McCartney when they saw little, cuddly Paul who was born on 18 June 1942.

No prophecy has ever been more fulfilled.

Not that you would have believed it during his teenage years, because he was quite fat. But he had that fatal charm that stayed with him, and whenever he got caught doing something wrong he could turn on the charm and generally get away with it, whereas brother Mike was always landing himself in trouble.

He also had a very stubborn streak (some things never change!) and as he learned to do everything left handed, his father tried to encourage him to use his right hand. But Paul wasn't having any of that, and when he began playing the guitar, he learned to play it with his left hand, which meant the guitar had to be strung upside-down.

His interest in music really took off at the age of 14. His mother was very ill at that time with cancer. She was operated on but didn't survive. The two brothers and their father pulled together and became even closer. That's when Paul began to pour all his energies into playing the guitar. It was the best therapy he could have had for coping with the loss of his mother.

Then Paul met George, and when they discovered how much they had in common they quickly became firm friends. How sad that during the break-up of The Beatles, the two who were the first to get together fell out the way they did. I don't believe George even attended the wedding of Paul and Linda.

Two days after the wedding, I watched sadly as Paul and Linda, along with Heather, drove out through the black gates and headed for Heathrow airport. They were taking a three-week holiday in New York to visit Linda's family.

I really did miss him terribly and so for the next three weeks there seemed little point in staying around Cavendish Avenue, although I passed by there every day because I worked and lived just down the road in St John's Wood. The neighbours must have been over the moon whenever Paul went away because there was a certain calm that descended on Cavendish Avenue with the absence of fans.

While in New York, Paul was spotted by a fellow-fan on 19 March, and she told me,

It was about eight in the morning when I saw Paul in Central Park, carrying Heather on his shoulders. He was staying on 83rd Street and I was there when he came home that evening. He'd been out all day and when he came back he found nine of us waiting for him.

First Linda climbed out of the cab, then Paul got out holding little Heather's hand. He seemed very pleased to see us and he was asking each of us, 'How are you? Are you all right? Nice to see you all.'

He looked really nice in baggy trousers, baggy jacket and yellow shirt. We asked if he'd pose for pictures and he said, 'Of course.' Then he went to the doorman and said to him, 'We're going out for the evening so we're going to need a babysitter for Heather.'

Then he noticed a little girl who'd come up to him holding out some flowers, and he said, 'Are they for me?'

Just then some girls came running across the road screaming and he told them not to scream. But he was very nice to everyone.

During this time there was very little Beatlewatching for me to do, although I did see George. But in the main they were all off doing their own thing – Ringo was filming *The Magic Christian*, John and his new bride Yoko were waging war on war and George had enough problems with those trumped-up drugs charges (as I'll explain later).

On 28 March, towards the end of Paul's vacation, I popped by his house to see Rosie, the friendly and kindly house-keeper who was always happy to tell me the latest news.

'When do you expect Paul back?' I asked mournfully.

'Either next Monday or Tuesday,' she replied, and my spirits rose.

The night before Paul returned home I saw lights on in his house for the first time since he'd left. It turned out that his brother Mike was in there, preparing some kind of welcome for Paul and Linda. But I didn't get to see Paul until the day after he got home. It was evening when I came face to face with him outside his house. He wore a blue shirt and looked gorgeous. I was immediately very shy and not sure what to say to him.

'Welcome home,' I said timidly.

He looked at me and smiled. 'Thank you,' he said, and went indoors.

Those early days of marriage to Linda still saw the old-style Paul, pleased to see his fans, and eager to please them. But he still had his moments when his mood would turn black. These were, after all, the immediate pre-split days when The Beatles were only just hanging in there together. His frustration at what was happening was bound to be unleashed on us, and I often found myself on the receiving end of a tongue-lashing from him. I suppose that was because I really made the effort to get as close to him as any fan possibly could, and even though I was on the outside of all that was happening, I saw perhaps more than most other fans just how varied his moods were. Of course, I had to remind myself that he was only human and perhaps it was unfair of me to not want him to change at all. Linda encouraged him to become more of a recluse and I'm convinced that his increasing intolerance towards the fans was because he wanted to protect her – though from what I could never say.

When the *Daily Mail* newspaper once interviewed me, I told them, 'I just want a relationship with Paul that would mean I don't have to stand by the gate. I'd like to be a friend.'

Instead, Paul became so distant, so hard to get through to, that I longed for yesterday.

CHAPTER SIX

Here Comes the Sun

I WAS OUTSIDE Apple with a group of other fans when the news came through about George's drugs bust. Sergeant Swain, the kindly doorman, came outside and told us that George had just received a phone call from his wife Pattie, telling him to come home immediately as the police were there with a warrant for their arrest.

We watched helplessly as George rushed out of the building to his waiting car and our hearts went out to him and Pattie as he sped home. He arrived to find the police playing Beatle records, drinking coffee and generally making themselves at home.

With Paul away in New York and with George very much on my mind, I decided to make the trek to George's house in the wilds of Esher. I say trek because when I got out at Esher station, there was a very long walk up the seemingly never-ending private road to George's house. And on this day snow was on the ground. The temperature was freezing, and I was exhausted by the time I got there. And should you ask if going to see a Beatle's house was worth all the aggravation, I'd reply, yes, it was worth it. If I hadn't thought it was, I wouldn't have stood outside in the freezing snow not knowing if I'd see George or not.

As I reached the house I saw his Mercedes parked in the garage so I knew he was at home, but I didn't expect necessarily to see him in person. His house was beautifully decorated with psychedelic designs, and on the side wall was written 'I love you' and 'Mick and Marianne were here' which I guessed might just have been personally inscribed by Mick Jagger and his then girlfriend Marianne Faithful.

I don't know if George spotted me roaming about his front yard or what, but he came outside and talked to me for over an hour. Eventually I found the courage to ask, 'Play something for me please, George.'

He smiled and said he couldn't today, but he didn't say it in any mean or unkind way. He was always so thoughtful and always seemed to find time for the fans. One evening outside Apple I asked him to sign my copy of the *Wonderwall* sound-track album. He never hesitated or said he didn't have the time as I've known other pop stars do. He just signed it, and the autographed record is something I really cherish.

George was and is so marvellous a person that it's no wonder the fans who worship him in particular, like Dominique, were willing to wait all night, every night, just to see him leave the EMI studios after an all-night recording session.

Of all The Beatles, George had the most stable upbringing, which must in many ways account for his more sober, maybe even mundane attitude during the mid-Sixties, which thankfully evolved into a positive, charitable look at life in later years. The thing was, having probably faced fewer difficulties as a young lad didn't allow him the luxury that the others had of releasing their frustrations and inhibitions on the stage. He was also the 'baby' of the group, born on 25 February 1943 in Liverpool (where else?) to Harold (a bus driver) and Louise.

As a boy he was always very independent. If he could do something himself, he would. When he was 14 he decided he wanted to buy a guitar – all the other boys in Liverpool seemed to have guitars. He bought one that was going cheap (no jokes please!) and he was really diligent in learning to play it. His mother was very supportive, telling him he could learn to play really well. And he did.

He created a group with his brother Pete and some friends and they auditioned to appear at the British Legion Club in Speke. When the stars of the show failed to appear George and his band went on instead and played right through the whole show. He had only formed the group so he could go to that audition, so that evening was the band's first and last performance.

His mother was always 100 per cent behind him, and when The Beatles became famous, she worked diligently behind the scenes, replying to the fans who wrote in from all over the world, and really did a great deal to help all of us get a little closer to The Beatles.

In America there was a huge national Beatles Fan Club with newsletters and pictures every month. She convinced her son to sign the first fan club charter in 1966, and had him autograph photos to give away in competitions. She was even instrumental in organizing the 'Harrison Herald', which was George's own monthly newsletter.

Certainly one of the biggest influences in George's life was Pattie. It was she who, as you know, encouraged George to try meditation, and that changed his life. They had married on 21 January 1966. Paul, his childhood friend, was his best man.

Of course, no one could have been a greater strength to George at the time of their arrest on drugs charges than Pattie, but my friend Lucy and I felt we wanted to at least show our support by going to the court-house when he and Pattie made their first appearance in court to answer the charges. It wasn't that we wanted to catch yet another glimpse of a Beatle. We simply felt we had to be there for him, and despite how corny and perhaps inconsequential that sounds, I believe it meant a lot to George to know we really cared.

That evening Lucy and I saw him at Apple and we said, 'Good luck to you, George.'

'Thanks for coming, girls,' he answered. And he meant it.

My own personal feelings about The Beatles taking drugs was one of abhorrence. I was so saddened when the news broke in 1966 that they were taking LSD and other narcotics. But I couldn't believe George was guilty of this drugs charge, and indeed the whole thing smacked of a frame-up.

The police had claimed that they had found traces of cannabis in a long peace pipe they found in George's house. The thing was, the pipe had been given to George as a gift while in India, and I believe him when he said he had no idea it had the remnants of someone else's cannabis in it. The police also found a nail file in Pattie's car that had traces of some narcotic on it, but Pattie insisted that the file had been given to her by some fan.

It seemed that the police were always hounding The Beatles, and George was the most vulnerable because he was caught up in the whole eastern culture where cannabis is as common as legalized narcotics (namely tobacco) are in the West.

On 31 March I saw George and Pattie again in court when they were fined £240 each. George then pleaded with the authorities to leave The Beatles alone. He rightly said that they'd done so much for their country and asked if it was too much to ask to be left alone.

Later I saw George again down at Apple. By now I suppose my face was becoming very familiar and he must have seen me in court because he said to me, 'How did you like the play?'

It had certainly been a farce. The authorities were simply making an example of George. But he didn't seem down-hearted – just relieved it was all over.

It seemed to me that of all The Beatles, George was the one at that time people most wanted to meet and shake hands with because no one could resist admiring him. How he has changed since those early years, when he proved to be the most moody member of the group and the one most likely to throw water over photographers.

From what I have observed, and speaking for myself also, the fans were far more tolerant towards George whenever he occasionally couldn't quite find enough time for us than we were towards Paul. There was so much respect for George. But then it must be said that he didn't have the problem Paul had of girls outside his house every day – because if you wanted to go to George's house, you really had to make an effort.

Even though I was a Paul fan, I hated it whenever George went away somewhere and I could hardly wait for him to return. He just has this incredibly strong personality and his inner soul, as Dominique observed, really does shine.

CHAPTER SEVEN

Act Naturally (But Don't Stop Playing Drums)

I SUPPOSE TO the tiny tots of today Ringo Starr is best known as the voice behind the children's TV series *Thomas The Tank Engine*. But to my generation he was first and foremost the most immediately recognizable drummer of any pop group of the Sixties (with the possible exception of Keith Moon of The Who, and I'm sure some will argue the point by naming various other drummers), and, second, he was a fast-rising movie actor.

Trouble was, by the time I came to London, his second career was rapidly overtaking his first, which perhaps exemplified more than anything else just how distant The Beatles were growing from each other.

I probably saw a lot less of Ringo than I did any of the other Beatles. He always seemed to be off somewhere filming. When he was back at Twickenham Film Studios making *The Magic Christian* with Peter Sellers and Raquel Welch, I did go there to see if I could catch sight of him. But for some reason or other I never saw him, although I must admit I didn't make an all-out effort to go down every day.

However, an Italian friend, Mirella, did make a determined effort to meet him in May 1969, when he was in Italy making a spaghetti western called *Blindman*. It was a very definite departure for him after all the typical Ringo Starr-type roles he had played in previous movies. In this one he was a sadistic Mexican bandit. Gone were the drums, the cheeky smile, the zany sense of humour and in their place was a six-shooter, a leer and a horse he was not exactly at home on.

Mirella told me:

Ringo had actually left Rome for a few days and came back accompanied by Mal Evans and another actor. Myself and two other girls were there to welcome him back. He seemed surprised to see us.

He said, 'Hi,' to us and shook our hands. He asked 'Where do you come from?'

I said I'd come from Florence just to see him.

He said, 'Well, that's nice of you.'

We saw him again on the Monday evening when he went to The Villa with a friend he had with him. Then we saw him the next morning, watching him learning to ride a horse for the film. He had a terrible cold and really was quite ill, but when he saw us he was very pleased and said, 'Hello, girls.'

First he rode on a white horse and then changed to a brown one. I'm afraid I don't think he could ride very well, but of course he had to for the film. Then he sat and chatted to us for a while and posed for some pictures with us. Although he didn't feel well he was in a very good mood.

We'd brought him a present – a belt. We gave it to him and he put it on. We were very, very pleased that he liked it.

He was complaining that he couldn't ride any of the horses properly. Then we gave him some mineral water to drink, and then he had to get back to work.

I saw him again at seven that evening back at the hotel and he was looking very, very tired.

That was the thing about Ringo. He seemed to suffer often with poor health. Born on 7 July 1940, he spent much of his childhood in and out of hospital. Consequently, he missed a good deal of schooling. When he was six he spent a year in hospital with peritonitis. He spent another whole year in hospital at the age of 13, this time for pleurisy.

During one hospital stay he and some other kids formed a makeshift band. There were four children bashing away on cymbals, another two on triangles, and Ringo on a toy drum.

During his teenage years, while he was working as an apprentice fitter, he helped to form a group called The Eddie Clayton Skiffle. They would perform for the other apprentices during the lunch break.

His gradual and increasing interest in music led to the break-up of his first real love affair. Since the age of 17, he had been dating a dark-haired upholstress called Gerry

McGovern. They were engaged for a year and planned to marry in March 1961, but when he was offered work at a Butlins holiday camp, she begged him not to go. He went to Butlins and she went her own way.

He joined The Beatles in 1962 after the other three decided Pete Best needed replacing. At the time Ringo actually had another offer to join a different band. He said with characteristically good humour that he joined The Beatles because they paid better!

One particularly ardent Beatle fan, Maureen Cox, used to be at The Cavern often to watch The Beatles perform. Ringo was her favourite. Before long she and Ringo were going together and that really caused a storm among Ringo's other fans. They ganged up on her and one day they attacked her while she was in a car. If she hadn't rolled up the window smartly, it's very likely that the jealous girls would have caused her real damage. She was six years younger than Ringo, but they were very much in love and on 11 February 1965 they were married at Colston Hall in London.

Their first son, Zak, was born on 13 September 1965, and they had a second boy, Jason, born on 19 August 1967.

Ringo's health continued to dog him. He missed the whole of the European tour of 1964 after he collapsed at a photographic studio, suffering from laryngitis and tonsillitis. He was taken to the University Hospital while a bewildered drummer called Jimmy Nicol found himself sitting behind the drums with the famous Beatles logo.

From his bed, Ringo said in an interview down the phone, 'There are hot water bottles all over the show and a lot of pretty nurses – but I'm still shivering!'

He was back in hospital at the end of the year to have his troublesome tonsils removed.

As I have said, Ringo was always the least affected by all that happened to The Beatles. Some have said that he has progressed the least, but I say that he has progressed as much as the others without changing. He has his finger in so many pies and his talent is really quite extraordinary. He can play drums, write music, sing, act, and hasn't been afraid of doing cabaret. Then, of course, there's *Thomas The Tank Engine* and he is also quite an inventor. But perhaps most important of all, he enjoys making people happy.

He hates arguing, believing it's much easier to be pleasant than unpleasant. He is certainly the most lovable of The Beatles, like a teddy bear. He likes people and once said, 'I like anyone who likes me.'

I'm afraid I never did have many encounters with Ringo. I usually only ever saw him going in and out of Apple or EMI, but he was always pleasant, and from what I gather from other people's experiences in meeting him, he has always been obliging, no matter what time it is or how tired he feels.

One evening a girl called Val and her two friends from America, Sher and Sarah, waited patiently outside the EMI studios in Abbey Road for Ringo to come out. He and George had both arrived together at about six and George was the first to emerge at 11 pm. The girls were beginning to wonder if the Beatle they'd come especially to see would ever come out.

Ringo finally appeared at midnight. He stepped outside carrying a guitar and strumming it as he came down the steps. Reaching the bottom step he let out a jubilant and long 'Goodnight!'

The girls had hoped he might stop and chat but he seemed intent on walking right past them and heading for home.

Sher spoke up, 'Wait a minute please, Ringo.'

'Yes?' said Ringo with a warm smile.

Val piped up. 'I've just bought your album *Beaucoup Of Blues* and I think it's just fantastic.'

'Thank you very much.'

'Can I have your autograph please?'

'Of course you can.'

As he was signing Sher asked him how his wife was. Maureen was expecting their third child, and Ringo said that she was well and that he was excited about having another baby.

Since that night Val was able to meet and talk to him on numerous occasions and she came to feel that he was her friend in a very real sense.

It's too bad there aren't more people like Ringo Starr. The world would be a happier place. And funnier.

CHAPTER EIGHT

Little Chance of Peace down Abbey Road

THE RIFT BETWEEN John and Paul was becoming quite evident. Where once The Beatles attended each other's weddings, John didn't turn up to see Paul wed Linda and likewise, on 20 March 1969, Paul wasn't there in Gibraltar to see John marry Yoko. Geographically, mentally, spiritually and creatively, John and Paul were, perhaps more than any of The Beatles, the furthest apart.

At that time it was still believed that not all was lost. The day after I welcomed Paul home from his New York vacation, Lucy and I were down at Apple when John and George came out and told us that there was the distinct possibility of The Beatles doing an American concert tour. Well, this just blew our minds – the very idea that The Beatles would perform live again was as eagerly anticipated as the Second Coming. Perhaps sensing our uninhibited excitement at the news, George stressed that it hadn't been fully discussed yet.

'If it happened,' he explained, 'it would probably be in California – John needs the money!'

Then one girl said, 'Will you play Texas again?'

'No, definitely not Texas,' replied George. 'They've nearly killed us every time we went there.'

What George said was definitely true of their 1965 Texas concert, when they were trapped on board their plane at Huston airport, the fans broke through the police barriers and literally swarmed all over the aircraft like bees round a queen.

Eventually a fork-lift truck arrived to lift The Beatles safely down from the plane and onto the tarmac where they had to run the gauntlet of shoes, cigarette lighters and handbags to get into their waiting car. From the safety of their hotel room John had exploded in anger at the fans' behaviour.

'We've no intention of being lynched,' he'd said.

And so if The Beatles were to play on American soil again, it wouldn't be in Texas.

Our frustration though was that we were in England, and Lucy piped up, 'What about playing in London?'

George smiled softly at her and said, 'Just for you, Lucy.'

That thrilled her so much she danced around on the pavement while George went on to tell us, 'The danger from the fans was one reason we stopped touring in the first place.'

At that John agreed that their greatest danger was from the fans. 'We don't want to put our lives at risk,' he said. In retrospect, that was a tragically ironic statement coming from him.

Along with Ringo, John was an extremely elusive Beatle. I never really got to meet him much, and frankly I don't think too many fans ever managed to get really close to him – spiritually that is, not physically, otherwise he would never have been so uselessly murdered more than a decade later.

He never slighted the fans. It's just that he wasn't around too much. He hardly ever seemed to be at home at his house in Weybridge but it was a place worth visiting because it virtually breathed with the Lennon *persona* of that time. On my way up there once I saw his Rolls pass by me twice, but whether or not he was in the car I couldn't tell. That was on my first visit to his house, and I was stunned by the serenity of the place. As opposed to the loud, psychedelic designs on George's place, John's was much more *avant-garde*. There were three statue heads outside the front door, and through the window I saw a life-size photograph of Yoko hanging up just inside the door. Beautiful yellow flowers grew at the front of the house and I gave in to the temptation of picking one. I still have it, pressed in one of my Beatle diaries.

Everything about John in those days seemed virtually to shout 'Peace and Love'. When he and Yoko married in Gibraltar they both wore white – he a suit and she a mini dress – and even their feet were adorned with white tennis shoes. But he never lost his sense of humour. When asked why he had picked Gibraltar for the wedding, John replied, 'It's British and friendly.'

The next day he and Yoko flew to Amsterdam where they positively invited ridicule from every quarter, but also the publicity he sought, when they staged their famous peace demonstration by staying in bed for a whole week. Reporters and photographers happily came and went to interview and snap what they considered to be a most bizarre couple.

Above the bed hung signs reading, 'BED PEACE' and 'HAIR PEACE'. Of course, the world laughed at them, but I, and thousands like me, admired John because we knew he was only doing the best he could to make the world sit up and take notice of what everyone knew to be true but didn't seem to be doing much about – making the world a safer place to live.

What the sneering onlookers never stopped to think about was that John Lennon was not a thick-skinned, cynical so-and-so, but a deep-thinking, highly sensitive person, who was really something of a genius at finding ways to reveal truths that surely we should all know but so often fail to recognize or accept.

Some of my friends have said to me, 'Why has John let us down when he was such a fantastic person before all this?'

I told them, 'John hasn't let us down. He is the one who was let down by fans and friends.'

The trouble was, there were those who couldn't bear to see John – who after all was always the most outspoken of The Beatles – finally express his innermost feelings that were always there but which only really surfaced when Yoko came into his life.

From the day he was born on 9 October 1940 to the day he died, John had to fight to get everything he wanted. There must have been times when he felt the whole world was against him. Even in 1969 he was still fighting, not with violence, but with reason, logic and a lot of love. Not that there was much love shown to him. During May he and Yoko found themselves locked out of the United States completely because they had a drugs charge hanging over them. But all John and Yoko wanted to do was present President Nixon, whose moral fibre we all know about, with an acorn as a gesture of peace.

Because John had become such a rare sight in London, I

consider it a special time whenever I did see him. It was almost an honour to catch a glimpse of him, whether it was outside EMI or at his own Savile Row Studios as I did on occasions.

What was really incredible was to see him up on the roof of Apple on 22 April 1969 at an official ceremony to change his name from John Winston Lennon to John Ono Lennon. It was up on that very roof that The Beatles had performed what was their very last and almost impromptu live performance for the *Let It Be* cameras. A crowd had quickly gathered in the street below to watch this now legendary mini-concert but once more the police stepped in to ruin everybody's enjoyment by stopping the show because, they said, The Beatles were causing a disturbance! There might have been more magic moments like that as I understand it, because The Beatles were apparently keen to do further free concerts in that wonderful, off-the-cuff manner, had the police not put a stop to it.

Maybe such rooftop performances might have saved The Beatles, but in a way that's almost too painful to contemplate.

An extra special time for me was when The Beatles recorded *Abbey Road* at the EMI studios. It began on 1 July 1969 and went on until the end of August. Every day, a crowd of us gathered outside the studios waiting for them to arrive, usually in the afternoon, and stayed until they left, which could be any time during the evening or late at night.

For me it was also a happy way of making friends with people from so many different countries. And they weren't all girls. German and French boys mingled with the rest of us, waiting and watching, hoping for an autograph or to take a picture.

The crowd became so large that often it was almost impossible to catch a fleeting glimpse of The Beatles. They flashed in and out of the studio to avoid being mobbed. It was all suddenly very much like the early days of Beatlemania because many times the fans surged forward to touch the still fabulous foursome, screaming and shoving.

Among the worst offenders were the European boys who behaved exactly like the girls, screaming and reaching out to

**Paul looking gorgeous, but he would
often shout at fans who pestered him**

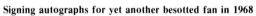

Signing autographs for yet another besotted fan in 1968

John — a man dedicated to peace and lov

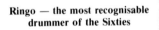
Ringo — the most recognisable
drummer of the Sixties

George — nicknamed the Sun King

Ringo's old home in Dingle, Liverpool

John's old home in Liverpool

Paul's old home in Liverpool

Paul's London home — 7 Cavendish Avenue

Part of George's home in Esher

Ringo's London home

The Beatles arrive at London Airport from Spain in 1965

Popperfoto

The bare emotions of a fan. We really did love The Beatles

Liverpool College of Art where John met Cynthia

Penny Lane — the street behind the song

Hysterical fans in 1966 at the departure of The Beatles for a tour of America *Popperfoto*

Standing outside the Apple Studios

The last Beatle movie *première* in London, 1970. None of The Beatles attended

Jane Asher

Pattie Harrison

Yoko Lennon

Linda McCartney

Popperfoto

Goodbye to all this *Keystone*

touch The Beatles. It seemed so odd to me seeing males react that way to other males. On one occasion the boys actually mobbed poor George who escaped somewhat shaken and probably just as surprised as I was.

There was certainly never a dull moment when there were a lot of fans around.

What really struck me at the time was just how rare it was to see all four Beatles on the same day. It was obviously a sign of the times although then I had no idea how close to breaking up The Beatles were. Of course, it wasn't surprising to see only Paul, George and Ringo turn up on the first day because the news quickly spread that John, Yoko, Julian and Yoko's daughter Kyoko had been injured in a car crash in Scotland, and although they escaped with only bruises and scratches, they were all admitted to hospital. But why John was in Scotland instead of beginning recording on *Abbey Road* was something you could only answer in retrospect. His heart just wasn't in The Beatles any more.

He and Yoko had put together their own band, called The Plastic Ono Band, and their first single, *Give Peace A Chance*, said it all. They had both been due at a press reception for their new record at Chelsea Town Hall, but still shaken by the accident they were substituted by Ringo and Maureen. By 7 July they were well enough to get The Plastic Ono Band together to sing *Give Peace A Chance* at the town hall, and after that I would have expected to see John at the Abbey Road studios.

But he didn't turn up for the new Beatles album until 17 July. It was certainly fantastic to see all four of them arriving at the studios. He looked well and there were no visible signs of any injuries.

Day after day I waited and watched, wondering how many and which Beatle would turn up. It must have proved an absolute headache for George Martin, who seemed rarely to have all four of them in the studio at one time.

A certain pattern of irregularity emerged. I noticed that from the outset, Paul turned up just about every day and often he was, from what I could see, the only Beatle there. After the first day, I didn't see George or Ringo until 11 days later. The day after that I counted only George.

Even after John made his bow on the *Abbey Road* session, I saw little of him going in or out. I remember seeing all four of them on 21 July but the very next day only John and Paul were visible. If any of the others turned up without my catching sight of them, if only fleetingly, they must have come and gone so fast that I missed seeing them only if I blinked.

My diary tells me that all four did work together on 28 July, but then it all became very spasmodic again. When I saw George for the first time for a while I remember actually thinking, well, that makes a change. Because for the most part he was preoccupied with producing recordings of *Hare Krishna Mantra* and *Prayer To The Spiritual Masters* at the Radha Krishna Temple in London with the Hare Krishna organization which he'd in fact signed to a contract.

As July turned into August Paul's commitment to the sessions seemed to slacken off. Even when he was there, or any of the others, I couldn't always be sure they were there to work on *Abbey Road* because each was so involved with other projects. For some months they had each worked individually at EMI on totally separate projects. Ringo, for instance, had played drums on *New Day* by Jackie Lomax who was under contract to Apple. At the same time Paul was producing Mary Hopkins' album *Postcard*, and George spent much of his time producing and playing guitar on Billy Preston's *That's The Way God Planned It* album.

By 1969 recording techniques were so sophisticated that I suppose it didn't really matter too much if anyone was missing. All the same, it was sad to realize that The Beatles were not wholly pulling together on what was their last recorded album (not the last released though, because the *Let It Be* LP was held up until the film was released, which wasn't until 1970). And when they did all turn up it was a bonus and a delight to know they were all actually under one roof.

Perhaps the man who had the biggest headache of all in dealing with the fans who gathered to see The Beatles each and every day was Sgt Swain, the kindly doorman at Apple who wrote the following poem which he called *Apple's Disciples, Passion Fruits.*

Whistling winds and falling snow,
Sweet young lovelies come and go
Like frozen waves upon the shore,
They push and sway outside the door.

They all flock here, all day and night.
Just like lost birds, they're in full flight.
And if a stranger should push in
Oh God, the uproar, what a din!
Until the stranger just gives in
And peace and quiet reign once again.

And when George Harrison leaves for home
In unison they sigh, 'Goodnight George, happy dreams,'
And with cameras held up high
They worship him just like a God
Who's dropped right from up high.

Then they in turn also move off
To wend their own way home
To go to bed and dream of George,
Each one dreams he's her own.

Sgt Swain (25/5/71)

CHAPTER NINE

I'm So Tired
(But Not Dead)

THE REAL PAUL MCCARTNEY died in 1966! That was the cheap
rumour that spread from New York in September 1969, when
a disc jockey announced over the air that an impostor who had
undergone plastic surgery and who spoke and sang like the
real McCoy (McCoytney?), had replaced the 'late' Beatle so
the group could continue making hits. Eventually that gossip-
mongering dee-jay was fired, but by then an almighty ruckus
had ensued.

When the *Abbey Road* album was released, the cover
photograph unwittingly added fuel to the fire as people
speculated on its meaning. The four Beatles were seen cross-
ing Abbey Road and dressed for a funeral, or so it was
conjectured. George was supposed to be the grave digger,
John the preacher, Ringo a mourner and Paul was the corpse.
This, many believed, was a vital clue in trying to fathom out
whether or not Paul was in fact already a corpse.

All I can say is, there was nothing phoney about the Paul
McCartney I knew. Nobody could have mimicked his varying
moods to such perfection. When he was in a good mood he
really was the sweet, lovable Paul the rest of the world usually
sees him as. But when he was in a bad mood, he could be
horrible. But then, I suppose I shouldn't blame him for some
of his tantrums because there were some girls who really
made his life hell.

There was one time during the summer of 1969 while he was
away when some unscrupulous girls managed to break into his
house and steal some of his personal colour slides. I had one
golden rule – I never went into any of The Beatles' homes. I
may have, on occasions, explored the grounds and gardens,
but I never went into the houses. I thought that kind of thing
detestable, so when I was given prints made from the slides, I
tried to give them to him. (I did, however, make black and

white prints of them first!) But he said he didn't want them so I got to keep them anyway. I suppose he might have thought that I was the one who stole the slides, but I don't think he did.

I don't know exactly who stole the slides, but a number of girls became angry with me for trying to give the prints to Paul because they figured I'd get them into trouble. So there were a few guilty consciences at least.

Because girls were managing to get inside his house when he was away, he began hiring guards to protect his property. I used to go and speak to them as they sat in the garage which became their larger-than-life sentry box. I became quite friendly with one of them, Charlie, an Irish fellow who sadly became very ill and passed away.

Towards the end of August Linda went into the Avenue Clinic Nursing Home to have her and Paul's baby. Just hours before the baby was due, Paul had numerous visitors including Twiggy and Justin, Julian Lennon, Neil Aspinal and the Metropolitan Police. Well, actually, the police didn't come to visit Paul but to see off all us girls. I never knew for sure who called the police at times like this, but I suspect it was usually the neighbours.

Baby Mary McCartney was born at 1.30 am on 28 August. I made several visits to the nursing home which was only a few blocks away from Paul's home, just so I could see the proud new daddy going in and out. A few days later I waited outside his house to watch him bring baby and mother back home. It was pitch black that night and I barely saw a thing. But out of the darkness I heard the cry of a baby, and from that time on Paul became more of a recluse than ever.

Not long after that I was with some other girls outside his gate. I guess some of them were playing around with his intercom, which at that time was still switched on, because suddenly out of the little loud speaker I heard his voice angrily shouting, 'Hello!'

I was so scared I ran away, not waiting to see what mood he was in. But I discovered just how cross he was the very next day as I watched Ringo arrive to visit baby Mary. Paul took one look at us girls and yelled, 'Go away!' I understand that the next day he was in a really foul mood, yelling at the girls, and I'm grateful I wasn't there for once. He was becoming increasingly intolerant of the fans and didn't try to hide it. One day I came in for a real scolding as I watched him walking up the avenue with Linda. It was so upsetting I just turned and walked away, but all the time he was yelling at me until finally he and Linda continued on their way.

The distance between Paul and his fans continued to grow, although we didn't let it deter us from waiting to see him. Almost every time we did, though, he told us off. One day in October he started having a go at one of my friends, Annet.

'Will you just go away,' he shouted at her, and then he looked at me and said, 'You too.'

Fortunately, there was no such hostility from George. I went to his home in Esher again and took photographs of his beautiful house, explored his grounds, saw his swimming pool and even took a peak through the window into his front room. After a while he and Pattie drove up in his Mercedes.

I said hello to him and asked him where he'd been. He said he and Pattie had been up to Apple, and he wasn't in the least put out at finding me and a few other girls roaming his property. The other girls got his autograph and I came away with a flower from his garden.

Apart from being much calmer and more charitably disposed than Paul, George didn't seem to be suffering the kind of turmoil that Paul was going through regarding the future of The Beatles. In fact, neither were Ringo or John, who each seemed to be off happily doing their own thing. But Paul, who worked separately from the others as well, producing and writing songs for people like Mary Hopkin, had always seemed the most optimistic about The Beatles and had at times come on very strong, judging by the film *Let It Be*, in trying to keep the four of them together. But suddenly, around this time, he lost the heart for it. He completely quit going to Apple.

It was some time before he finally phoned the Apple offices, saying that he was 'nervous and uncertain of things'.

One thing had just led to another. Previously both Ringo and George had expressed their desire to leave the group and indeed they had both walked out, if only temporarily, during the recording of *The Beatles*, which fans called *The White Album*. At least in January of 1969 there had seemed some hope when George, Ringo and John seemed intent on keeping everything going when they expressed their wishes to bring in Alan Klein to run things, but Paul had been against Klein from the start, wanting Linda's father and brother to handle Apple's affairs. When Klein was actually installed as their manager, Paul protested loudly. He just didn't trust Klein. Things got worse when, in September, John said that he wanted to quit The Beatles.

Now, with Paul staying away from Apple, the end of The Beatles seemed quite certain. It didn't help that the 'Paul is dead' rumour persisted. At the beginning of November a friend from the United States, Kris, wrote to me telling me how shocked she was to hear my voice coming over the air on the radio in an interview with disc jockey Alex Bennett of MCA. He'd come over from New York to London to investigate the rumour and had interviewed a number of fans, including me. I had angrily said to him, 'How can you prove he is dead?'

But the rumour, unlike the real Paul, didn't die. American singers began recording songs in remembrance of Paul. José Feliciano recorded *Dear Paul*, Terry Knight made, *Saint Paul*, The Mystery Tour recorded *The Ballad Of Paul* and Billy Shears and the All Americans recorded *Brother Paul*. The only positive side to all this was that sales of Beatle records went twice as high as normal.

With all that was going on, Sergeant Swain, the Apple doorman, wrote this poem.

> What's happened to Paul McCartney?
> He's in the news again.
> Is it true or just a rumour
> That he's left us once again?
>
> In the past the world kept asking
> Is it true that Paul is dead
> The phones they kept me busy
> Nearly drove me off my head.
>
> Now once again the phones are ringing
> Asking, 'Is it true?

That Paul has just quit Apple,
If anyone should know, it's you!'

I told them all, 'I'm just the guard'
Referred them all to you,
Oh Mavis Smith I wish you luck
I know that you'll pull through.

But if your head should start to ache
Then my advice to you
Is drink a glass of Epsom Salt
And pass your trouble through.

Paul wasn't totally inactive though. He had been busy writing and producing the single *Come And Get It* by Badfinger, one of the groups under contract to Apple. The song was from Ringo's film, *The Magic Christian*, so in some ways there was still collaboration between some Beatles. But for the most part they were all going off in different directions. George went on tour backing Delaney and Bonnie.

John hit the headlines again in November when he sent back his MBE. He said that when The Beatles accepted their awards in 1965, he had been against the idea but went along with it because Brian Epstein wanted them to. He sent it back, he said, because The Plastic Ono Band's single *Instant Karma* had slipped in the charts; but more than that, it was because the Americans shouldn't have been in Vietnam.

It was all part of his peace plan and it seemed an appropriate time to send back his award. His aunt Mimi said that if she'd known he was going to do that she would have hidden it!

Back in Cavendish Avenue, the fans continued to wait and watch for any sign of Paul, but he was rarely seen. In December a curious incident occurred to a bunch of girls. (By this time the fans were already split into 'the troubles' and 'the goodies'.)

The two factions sat apart from each other on a long wall opposite Paul's house. It was a bitterly cold evening and the girls sat huddled together in their separate groups.

A red Mini car approached from down the avenue and pulled up where the girls sat. Out jumped a man and woman, one holding a camera, the other with a flash light which shone brightly on the girls' faces.

'Let me see your faces,' cried the man. The girls tried to hide behind their hands and long hair but already the camera was clicking madly.

One girl knew she had had her picture taken before she could hide her identity. They all feared their pictures would appear in the next morning's newspapers. Some girls ran away but among those who stayed behind was a girl who was suddenly prodded sharply by a shooting stick held by one of the 'Press' people.

It turned out, though, that the man and woman were merely occupants of Cavendish Avenue out to try and scare the girls into giving up their vigil. It was a mean trick and didn't work anyway. I'm sure Paul had nothing to do with it.

There was still some excitement reminiscent of the old Beatle days. On 15 December I went to the very first concert given by The Plastic Ono Band in aid of UNICEF.

There were a number of supporting acts and before John and Yoko's band came on the MC said that there was a special guest to perform with The Plastic Ono Band. The rumour quickly spread that it might be another Beatle, and sure enough, when it was announced that it would be George Harrison, the whole audience went wild.

Well, at least half of the famed quartet were on stage again.

It turned out to be an incredible evening. Billy Preston, Eric Clapton and Keith Moon were among the famous artists in The Plastic Ono Band. John hadn't lost any of his magic. His magnetism on stage was totally captivating. He had long, flowing hair, and both he and Yoko were dressed in white.

Back down Cavendish Avenue things were depressing. I hardly ever saw Paul and when I did he was usually telling me and any others who were there to go away. On one occasion he was giving Sandra and myself one of his usual lectures about hanging around outside his house. What he didn't know was that Sandra had her tape recorder turned on and was recording everything. Even if it was just a telling-off, at least she had his voice on tape for posterity.

I had been in London less than a year and had made every effort to be supportive, friendly and pleasant. During the early months, I had bought Paul a present which at the time he'd graciously accepted. At one time he said to me and another girl that we were his friends.

Of all The Beatles I still loved Paul the most and although I came to realize that I could never be anything more to him than a dedicated fan, I never gave up trying to be his friend.

But by the end of 1969, and as intent as I was to still remain loyal, he had changed so much in such a short space of time, it's almost as though the old Paul McCartney really was dead.

CHAPTER TEN

All Things Must Pass
(Even The Beatles)

IT HAD BECOME quite rare to see Paul at Apple, but on the third day of 1970 he was actually there with George and Ringo. This seemed like a good sign, to know that three Beatles were together under one roof, but whether their meeting together was amicable or not I couldn't know. This was, after all, only three months before Paul announced he was leaving The Beatles so I would guess that there was much discussion, perhaps even heated, going on about The Beatles' affairs, which were now in the hands of Alan Klein whom Paul was unhappy with.

That evening I saw Paul leave the EMI studios in Abbey Road where he was working on his first solo LP *McCartney*. It was about ten past twelve and very few people could have known he was there as there were very few fans waiting outside. I followed at a discreet distance as he, with Linda clinging tightly to his arm, walked home. Then I went back to the studios to wait for George, who I knew was there.

Poor George! When he came out he tripped down the steps but he wasn't hurt. He was as cordial as ever. Thank God for George Harrison.

The next day George, Paul and Ringo were recording at EMI. The evening had begun with my friends and I walking towards Paul's home when to our surprise we saw him and Linda cutting across their lawn and out into the street. Linda was accompanying him to EMI every time now, it seemed. They crossed the road and stopped to buy some magazines and newspapers. I knew he was going to head down Abbey Road so I walked ahead of him towards the studio. As he approached I stood with my back to him. I wanted to watch him but I just didn't want any hassle, but I did turn around to see him and Linda going up the steps and into the recording studios.

A few minutes later George, who must have seen me through a window or something, came out and called to me from the doorway.

'Thanks for the flowers you sent,' he said.

I nearly died, it was such a beautiful moment. It was so typical of George to make an acknowledgment like that.

I hung around and they finally emerged at about three-thirty in the morning. When Ringo saw the small gathering of fans he said, 'My, you must be strong people to wait so long out in the cold.'

I never saw John around this time because he was in Copenhagen with Yoko where they were having their long hair cropped short as one of their gestures towards the peace movement. Shortly after this, Ringo also had his hair cut short.

I know that there are many who scoffed at John and Yoko's gesture, but they really were serious in everything they did in trying to bring peace to the world. Late in 1969 they had begun their world-wide peace campaign in earnest, by erecting huge billboards proclaiming peace in 12 cities around the world, as well as having thousands of smaller posters put up around the suburbs of places like London, Rome, New York, Athens and Tokyo.

Considering all they were trying to do, the scoffers might have stopped and expressed a little sympathy for the couple when, in February, Yoko lost the baby she was expecting. It was her third miscarriage.

Back in London, Beatlewatching continued at Apple, in Abbey Road and along Cavendish Avenue, not always with pleasant results. One evening I saw Paul arrive home in his Continental Rolls. I just turned and began walking away as I had come to expect what his response to any welcome would be. And sure enough, he told two other girls to 'Go away'. He hadn't changed.

It seemed that by this time The Beatles themselves had become bored with The Beatles. And perhaps, as sad as this was to fans, it shouldn't be so difficult to understand in retrospect because of all the internal tension and disharmony that had arisen. While in Hollywood to promote *The Magic Christian* Ringo faced 200 members of the Press to talk about

his new film. When continually probed about the future of
The Beatles, Ringo, normally so good natured, retorted,
'This is supposed to be a press conference to promote my new
film. The other Beatles aren't here, so I don't want to be
answering questions for them.'

Just how contentious things had become among members
of the group no one on the outside could have envisioned.
Derek Taylor told Mike Munn,

> The whole thing about the break-up of The Beatles was
> absolutely horrendous. It was an awful time for them
> because where the boys had once been so close and such
> good friends, there they were falling out with each other.
> Although now of course they that survive are all good
> friends again.
>
> If John were still alive I think it's very possible the four of
> them would have performed again – not as The Beatles, but
> as some sort of super-group with other musicians, probably
> for something special like Live Aid. It would have had to be
> something special like that to bring them back together
> again. But that's all so hypothetical we shouldn't even be
> thinking it.
>
> I think it's true to say that everything that happens ends
> in a horrible way. It was inevitable that The Beatles would
> end in such a horrible way.

Just how horrible, nobody in the earliest months of 1970 could
contemplate. The division in the group was still not generally
publicly known. It was only when the film *Let It Be* was
released, after Paul said he was leaving the group, that those
on the outside were able to get any idea of how bad things
were creatively and personally between them. And even then
the film was edited so that some of the more personal conflicts
weren't too apparent.

During the days leading up to the split the sight of more
than one Beatle together became ever more rare. And to see
Paul with any of The Beatles had suddenly become a thing of
the past. By this time I had already begun work on my
intended book about The Beatles and took the opportunity to

ask George if there was any way I might get some 'inside' help with it.

'I'll make an appointment for you to see one of the personnel at Apple called Mavis Smith,' he promised.

He kept his promise. On 2 March I saw him outside Apple with Mal Evans. He turned to Mal and said, 'Make sure Carolyn gets into Apple tomorrow to see Mavis.'

The next day I was in. It was incredible just to be inside Apple for the first time. I met Mavis Smith and told her about my book but have to admit that no positive results came from that meeting. I did get to see Paul who must have wondered what I was doing inside Apple.

Being on the inside for once did give me an idea of the amazing organization that had been set up, but what was evident was the amount of activity and interest in The Beatles' individual works as opposed to the group as a whole. At that time the only matter with anything to do with a Beatles collaborative effort concerned the release of the *Let It Be* film and album which had had its fair share of problems. The record was supposed to be a 'new Beatles phase' album, featuring the group playing 'live' without the use of effects in any way. But although the live performances were in the film, some of the tracks had to be rerecorded and reproduced for the album. Initially, for instance, a female choir had been used to back Paul for his number *The Long and Winding Road.* Paul was so disappointed with the results that he called in Phil Spector to change it.

Some of 'the troubles' were still giving Paul a hard time. To celebrate his first wedding anniversary a bunch of girls decided to pull another of their pranks that evening. They lined up some of Paul's dustbins on his drive-way. Seeing what was happening, one of the neighbours called the police who arrived in time to catch the girls red-handed. Charges were actually brought against the girls this time. I'm glad I was further up the road out of harm's way otherwise, although I had nothing to do – and wouldn't have anything to do – with pranks like that, it's likely I might have been rounded up with 'the troubles' and charged too.

The fact is, I always tried to steer clear of any trouble, which was why in recent weeks I avoided as much as I could coming face to face with Paul. It was never my intention to hassle him in any way but I still dearly wanted to be his friend. I guess I'm a coward at heart but more than that, I was brought up on the Christian creed of 'Love thy neighbour'. And I certainly loved Paul. I wouldn't have done anything to hurt him, unlike some of the other girls.

Even if The Beatles had intended to work together again, they would have found it awfully hard to find the time. John and Yoko were heavily involved in their peace campaign as well as their own band; Ringo was spending a great deal of time in America and even guest-starred on the Laugh-In TV show; George spent much of his time in March producing *Givinda* by the Radha Krishna Temple; and Paul was busily engaged in his own creative work, producing another Mary Hopkin song and performing solo on a London Weekend Television show, singing *Maybe I'm Amazed*.

On 7 April I decided to face Paul and show him that I still cared and that I wasn't intent on causing him any trouble. As he arrived home I presented him with a huge sunflower.

He seemed genuinely touched and said 'Thank you.' This was more like the old Paul McCartney and I was over the moon about it.

A little while later, that same evening, Rosie, Paul's housekeeper, came out and told me that Paul and Linda were having a furious row about me. I suppose she objected to him accepting my token gift and this made me realize that, despite his moods and tantrums, he really did care about the fans and that he didn't really consider me a threat. After all, I had never been involved with any of the terrible things some of the other fans had done, and I did try and give him the prints of those stolen slides of his. I had visions of being able to continue watching and waiting for him without further scoldings.

The very next day I waited for hours to see Paul arrive home. But he never showed up. I began to get a feeling that something was terribly wrong. The following evening I was there waiting for him when he came home. To my horror he began telling me off again. It was so horrible and unexpected. It was the old usual thing about how I shouldn't hang around his house. I couldn't understand his sudden shift of mood. He seemed so intense and ill at ease.

The next day I realized the cause of his outburst. It was 10 April 1970. The day Paul McCartney announced he had quit The Beatles.

It was more distressing than the news of his marriage more than a year earlier.

He made a statement, saying that he wasn't sure if his break with the group was temporary or permanent. There was just so much conflict between the once Fab Four and he just didn't get along with the other three, especially with John. He said that each of the group now had their own families and life-styles and their future together had been very vague for some time.

He had decided that he would be the one to take the first big step away from the group. And although he said that he didn't know if his decision was final, he must have felt deep-down inside that he would never go back. Over the past couple of years the other three members had each made a temporary break from the group. Paul was the one who made it permanent.

There was no way we, the fans, could accept that the most important thing in our lives had come to an end. On 11 April we congregated outside Apple in the vain hope of seeing Paul and hearing him retract his statement about the break-up. But when it became apparent Paul wouldn't show up at Apple, we went down to his house and gathered there.

Someone who didn't approve of us at all – possibly someone on the inside, I suspect – called the police. This time I wasn't quick enough to escape and my name was taken down and I was given a warning.

I was scared enough by that warning, as well as by Paul's now intense intolerance of us, to ensure I kept out of his way the next day. I watched as he came out with some visitors and when he said goodbye to them I quickly made myself scarce. Not being very brave, I wanted to avoid any further trouble and couldn't bear to see him lose his temper. The whole atmosphere was tense and it was so hard to adjust to.

For the most part, Paul stayed locked away in his home

immediately following the news of his leaving The Beatles. He felt he had a pretty good excuse for being such a recluse at this time because he was working on his first solo LP *McCartney*. But he sometimes went walking down the street and around the corner to the EMI studios, usually taking his whole family with him. It seemed a good idea to try and keep out of his way, but I still wanted to be able to see him so I kept at a discreet distance.

Let It Be was finally *premièred* on 20 May, and I managed to get tickets for it at the London Pavilion, the scene of all the previous Beatles' *premières*. But it was a disappointment to all the fans who lined the streets when not one of The Beatles showed up, although Jane Asher, Cynthia Lennon and Richard Lester did. It was strange that those three people, who were once such a major part of The Beatles, should be there.

The film was also *premièred* on the same night in Liverpool and New York, but still no Beatles turned up. I happen to know that George was in New York at that time because a girl called Carol wrote to me, saying that she had discovered the place where he was staying while there on business.

She told me how she made up her mind to go to his private flat and try to meet him. She went with a bunch of friends, and when they knocked on his door, he cordially greeted them and said, 'Come on in, girls.'

They sat themselves down on the couch and he perched on the edge of the coffee table, talking to them for a full 20 minutes. Said Carol, 'He was really sweet.' Which is exactly how I'd expect George to be.

I next saw George back in London on 27 May when he came out of EMI at about midnight. People have often asked me, 'Was it really worth hanging around until all hours of the morning just to see a Beatle?' My response is, it was always worth waiting all those hours, especially to see George because at that time of the morning he was always in such a lovely mood. No one could ever imagine the feeling he gave us with just a little smile. It made all those hours of waiting so worthwhile.

At that time George was working on his first major solo album – the three-record set of *All Things Must Pass*. He'd taken a back seat creatively as a Beatle for so long, he was obviously enjoying himself hugely. He continued to work on the triple album through into July and since Paul was in Scotland and John and Ringo were hardly ever around, I went most days to wait for George in Abbey Road. He usually arrived at the studios around five in the afternoon or some-times as late as seven, and then worked all through the night. He would turn up looking as gorgeous as ever, smiling and waving to us. He continued this pattern until 7 July when his wonderful mother, Louise French Harrison, died of a malig-nant tumour. He was at her bedside when she passed away in the Chatterbridge Hospital in Cheshire. She had been in hospital for some time, receiving radiation treatment for a cancerous brain tumour.

In memory of Mrs Harrison the George Harrison Fan Club set up the Louise F. Harrison Memorial Cancer Fund, raising money for the Chatterbridge Hospital to help other cancer victims.

She was buried on 20 July. George poured himself into his work, continuing to record *All Things Must Pass* as well as producing with the Radha Krishna Temple. He was always willing to give a helping hand wherever needed and he split his time between recording at EMI and going down to Trident Studios in Soho.

I used to go to Trident to see him there. Usually he'd arrive at about two in the afternoon and work until six the following morning. There were always girls waiting for him in the cold, early hours and he'd always emerge looking like he'd only just risen from bed after a good night's sleep, not like he'd have to face a long journey home after an all-night session in the studios. He was just fantastic.

One day in August he came out on to the steps of EMI and talked to me and some other girls who were there for over an hour. He asked us if we wanted any coffee, and he just chatted away. If only Paul could have been like that.

Paul had left for his farm in Campbeltown in June. It was hardly the kind of place a horde of fans was going to swarm over, so it seemed a good idea to make the long trip up to Scotland myself along with a friend, Anne. We thought that he couldn't object to two such devoted fans buying a ticket to ride all that way just to see him.

It wasn't as though we were just making a day trip of it. The coach trip took 18 hours in all and we arrived in Campbeltown at three pm on 27 June. We booked into a bed-and-breakfast and then set out to find Paul's farm.

We were driven part of the way by a fellow who used to escort Paul around when he first started coming up to Scotland. Then we began an hour-long walk up the hill to the farm. As we approached the farm, we began to wonder just whether we ought perhaps to turn around and go back, because we'd not exactly found favour with him the last time we saw him in London. But we figured it was too late to turn back now so on we went.

In the distance we could make out figures moving. Since I'm rather near-sighted, I wasn't able to make them out very clearly, but Anne could see very well – and, sure enough, they were Paul and his family. Anne gave me a running commentary on what was happening.

Not long after we saw a jeep approaching and we both feared that it might be Paul coming to chase us off. But it turned out to be a nice man whom I came to know quite well, called Mr McDougal. He was Paul's neighbour. We'd heard that he was supposed to be quite an ogre, but he turned out to be very sweet and we had quite a pleasant chat with him.

After he left we chickened-out of going any further towards the farm and headed back to our bed-and-breakfast lodgings.

The next day we decided we'd get much closer to the farm. We had to walk the whole distance this time and it took us two hours in the pouring rain. As we staggered along the long and winding road we saw lambs in the fields about us. We trudged on, up and down hills, round umpteen bends, keeping to the narrow road the whole time instead of cutting across the fields as we had done the previous day.

Eventually we came to a wooden gate. Beyond that was Paul's farm. And there was Paul himself, digging in a square patch of dirt. Linda came out of the house and saw us standing on the opposite side of the gate. All we were doing was standing there, watching Paul at work. She went up to him, said something and then he turned and saw us. They both approached us. He did not look pleased to see us, as we should have expected.

He was immediately seized by an impulse to be rude and insulting which did surprise us really because we hadn't expected him to be quite so bad. Neither did we really expect him to welcome us with open arms.

'You're just like animals,' he said.

'We don't want to cause any trouble,' I said. We tried to reason with him but he just got worse.

He said, 'Look, I've retired. You're acting just like seven-year-olds. I suppose when you leave here you'll start talking about me and saying how gorgeous and sweet I am in spite of the way I'm talking to you now.' He seemed unable to talk to us in any reasonable tone. 'You're just standing there, swooning over me,' he said.

'We really only want to be friendly, honest,' we explained.

'Well, you're not going about it the right way. If you really want to be my friends you'll stay away from me.'

'We thought that when you like someone you want to be with them.'

Well, it was just a waste of breath. It seemed to me that he was intent on driving everyone away from him. We tried desperately to get through to him and said, 'If you've retired, are you going to remain in Scotland?'

'Mind your own business!'

Well, Paul was definitely wrong about one thing – we didn't leave there saying how sweet and gorgeous he was!

But I wasn't deterred from trying to show him that I really cared and didn't want to hassle him. I really missed him whenever he was away and just wanted to see him, if only for a few minutes. So, finding the courage and the fare up to Scotland, I returned to Campbeltown on 11 September, this time with a different companion, Dolores. It seemed a good idea at the time (as most ideas do) to go immediately to the farm before our courage failed us. Unfortunately, it was quite dark, but that gave us the cover we needed to make it all the way to Paul's front door – almost. We must have made too much noise because Linda opened the door just before we got to it.

'Oh, it's Carolyn,' she said, and she didn't make it sound like it was a pleasant surprise.

That unnerved me and I stumbled in the dark. Splosh! I suddenly found myself standing knee-deep in a stream that we hadn't seen directly in front of us. And that was about the extent of my second outing to Campbeltown.

Back in London, I decided to try and find a live-in job close to Paul's house. A local domestic agency found me just such a job in Cavendish Close, around the corner from Paul's house, working for Sir and Lady MacFadean.

A few days later, while Paul was still farming in Scotland, I saw George at Apple. He was talking about Paul, and it all sounded very ominous. He said that if The Beatles were to record again, they would need a new bass guitarist. Feelings against Paul were running quite high among the rest of the group. When I saw Ringo some days afterwards, he was in a bad mood – one of the very few times I'd ever seen him like that.

But the three Beatles who remained friends did seem intent on working together still. At the end of September 1970 John and Yoko returned from Los Angeles, where they'd been living, to start work on their own album. I was delighted to see John arrive at the EMI studios with George and Ringo who were, I assume, lending support to the Plastic Ono Band's new project. George was also just finishing off his *All Things Must Pass* recording sessions.

One day I went down to Paul's house – he was still in Campbeltown – to visit one of the guards. The security guards were never allowed inside Paul's house and had to remain in the garage. Paul's green Continental Rolls was keeping the guard company. It was very quiet as there were no girls hanging around and out of the silence both the guard and I were dumbstruck when we heard the unmistakable sound of the chief security officer. If he'd found me there both I and the guard would be for the high jump.

'Quick!' cried the guard in alarm, 'into the boot of the car.'

I clambered in and the guard shut the boot. There was a click and I knew I was locked in. I felt as if I was in there for an eternity, but it was only a few minutes. The guard chatted with his boss, all the time wondering if I was suffocating. I think he half expected to drag me out semi-conscious.

When his boss finally left him, he fumbled to unlock the boot. Maybe he was panicking because he had trouble getting the boot open again. After a few more minutes the top came up and I emerged a little hot and breathless but alive, to both mine and the guard's relief.

John was down at EMI to celebrate his thirtieth birthday. George and Ringo were with him. Paul wasn't. There was obviously quite a shindig going on inside. George had arrived carrying a bouquet of flowers for his Beatle friend. It was ironic that at the very beginning of Beatle history George and Paul had become firm friends while the young John Lennon had been reluctant to accept the even younger George Harrison. Now here they were, firm friends for the rest of John's life.

It was frustrating for us girls to have to remain outside EMI and the party, but The Beatles didn't forget us. John had Mal Evans bring some of his birthday cake out to distribute among us.

One advantage I had over the other fans was that, having been introduced previously into the Apple combine thanks to George, I was welcome inside once again. During October I met Derek Taylor which is a welcome and pleasing experience in itself, because he went through so much of what The Beatles went through and knew them as well as anyone. He remains firm friends with the surviving Beatles and numbers George Harrison among his very best friends.

Inside Apple, I was introduced to James Taylor who was an Apple recording artist at that time. Afterwards he walked me down to the underground station and even paid my fare. I was able to go back to Apple a few weeks later to view a short Beatle film that showed them performing *Hello Goodbye*, *Strawberry Fields* and *A Day In The Life*. It also contained footage about the time Brian Epstein died. Considering all that had happened, it was both exciting and poignant.

I went back to Apple not long after to see Derek Taylor and stayed for about four hours, during which time I saw Ringo a couple of times. I'm glad to say he was in better spirits. But the air was thick with tension, as though something was about to burst. It wasn't long after that that the biggest pop bubble of all time did burst.

The Beatles were in the doldrums, but Beatlemania was still alive. One fan, Anne, told me about the day she and two friends, Chris and John, left Waterloo Station late one afternoon in November of 1970, hoping to see George at his home in Esher.

I sat clutching a bouquet of three carnations which I'd bought for George – well, carnations are very expensive, you know! We talked and joked the whole time we were on the train about how George would probably be kind and friendly, and we hoped he would talk to us for ages and maybe even give us a ride back to the station in his Mercedes.

When we got to Esher, we walked all the way to his house which took for ever, and walked boldly up to his door and knocked. It was exciting and frightening at the same time.

George answered the door and I handed him the flowers. He thanked me for them and then John asked if he could take some photos and George said, 'Yes.'

After he posed for John he said he had to go out later and had to say goodbye. We decided to wait by the gate to watch him go and as time passed we watched as the lights in George's house went on and off mysteriously. We never did find out why that was.

Finally Chris and John said they were going to the garage but being a coward I said I'd wait at the gate. I kept peering round the gate to see what was going on until finally I saw George come out of his house. After a while I heard two car doors slam and I thought, it couldn't be Chris and John getting in his car!

Then I saw George driving his car down the drive and as he reached the bottom of the drive I had the shock of my life. In the car sat John and Chris – Chris was in the front passenger seat next to George. For a moment I thought he wouldn't stop for me, but he did, and I got in the back seat next to John.

Then we drove off and went like the wind. Chris was giving George directions how to get to the station – I guess George had never used the train service and didn't know how to get there. We were absolutely hysterical when we got out of the car. It was like the end of a beautiful dream.

Towards the end of the year Paul wasn't in Scotland the whole of the time. That winter saw him often in New York. A fan from the Big Apple saw him in that city about 25 times during 1970. The last time had been in December. He was looking out through a window of the Stanhope Hotel, watching the Women's Lib parade. She said he was 'just beautiful with his tan and full beard. He looked exactly like he did in *Let It Be*.'

She told me that five of her girlfriends also saw Paul on Hallowe'en. He had entered into the spirit of the whole thing and was dressed in some spooky costume. They went up to him and he went 'Boo!' right in their faces.

But not all the New York fans were overjoyed with the way he often slighted them. Kris said,

We didn't like the way he had treated us so, the night before he left New York, about a dozen of us decided to stare at him when he came outside – just stare. Nobody would take any pictures or talk to him.

When he came out you wouldn't believe the silence. None of us stirred. He walked out quite slowly, looking at each of us and he looked so sad – like he wanted to say 'Why aren't you following me?'

Then I regretted what we were doing – it really hit him. I didn't think he had much emotion left until this night. He got in the taxi cab and he kept looking around at us, but we all just stood there and stared with these really serious looks on our faces. Well, he was three-quarters of the way down the street and we just couldn't contain ourselves any longer. We jumped up and down, shouting 'We did it!' We made a noise like thunder – he must have heard it. Well, maybe he did; who knows? Then, deep-down inside, we felt we didn't really want to do what we just did.

I used to go to the studio where he was doing some recording every day. Any day could be the last. Lots of times he was smiling a lot. He'd say, 'Good evening, girls, see you tomorrow.'

At the hotel when we were there I think he really understood us. There would only be four or five of us, and he said, 'Listen, would you do me a favour while we're in New York. Nobody knows where we are and we'd like to keep it that way.'

We told him, 'All we want to do is talk to you.'

So Paul said, 'I understand you want to stop and have a chat, but I'll do all that at the studios.'

My friend Claudia said, 'Is that a promise?'

And Paul said so solemnly like he really meant it, 'That's a promise.' Then he said, 'See ya' and left.

One day I bought some liquor for him. There were only four of us waiting as he got out the cab. He looked so cute and boyish still. He was wearing a red turtle-neck sweater and an okay blue suit. One of the girls, Evy, went up to him and handed him the liquor I'd bought. I'd chickened-out of giving it to him. Anyway, he jumped back as though surprised and said, 'Is this for me?' He looked at the bottle and exclaimed, 'Wine?' He then said, 'Thank you,' and he literally bounced his way into the studio. He was just like the old Paul. But he wasn't always that nice.

Kris always kept a look-out for any Beatle who happened to be in New York. One day she saw Ringo playing with his sons, Zak and Jason. She said it was like seeing a magazine spread come to life. Ringo's family increased in November 1970 when his baby daughter Lee was born.

As for John and Yoko, people had started to sit up and take notice of them. They were appearing on various American TV chat shows and I think that made a big difference to the attitudes of many towards them.

George was proving very successful as a solo artist. His hit single *My Sweet Lord* had been released and was doing well. In later years, he was to be sued for plagiarism over that song. But George didn't have to cheat because he is such a brilliant composer. Just listen to his contributions to Beatle recordings like *I Me Mine, For You Blue, It's All Too Much, Don't Bother Me* and the beautiful *Here Comes The Sun*. As for *My*

Sweet Lord, it's unique and only vaguely resembles the song *He's So Fine* that he's supposed to have pinched the tune from. The only thing George ever stole in his life was a little thunder from Lennon and McCartney.

On 31 December, everything hit the fan. Paul McCartney filed suit against The Beatles. He was seeking legal dissolution of The Beatles' partnership against George, Ringo and John.

He must have been working up to this for weeks, and I suppose in the light of this knowledge it's quite understandable why Paul was so uptight with the fans and especially with me. But it didn't prepare me for the blackest day in my life when I came face to face with Paul in an incident which brought my Beatlewatching days to an end.

CHAPTER ELEVEN

I Should Have Known Better (But I Didn't)

I'M NOT MAKING any accusations against Paul McCartney. I did that 17 years ago and it got me into more trouble than I'd ever been in or ever hope to be in again. In fact, it would be far easier for me just to leave out this whole episode of my life. But what happened between Paul and me in Campbeltown in 1971 was the very thing that brought my Beatlewatching days to an end and coincided with the final curtain on The Beatles and Beatlemania.

Before I tell you about the 'alleged incident', as the police and newspapers called it at the time and for which no charges were ever brought against Paul, let me say that I don't hold Paul responsible for what happened. After all, I've had 17 years to think about it and if I'm to be totally honest about the whole sorry episode, I have to admit that I'd finally gone too far in trying to do nothing more than show my love and devotion for my most favourite of all The Beatles.

It's a case of 'if I knew then what I know now' I never would have gone to the police to charge Paul with assault – besides, the Procurator Fiscal never believed me anyway; and I never would have believed certain newspaper reporters who made out they were on my side and took me before Paul, face to face, and told him to apologize, because in doing so they only made Paul the victim as well as me; and, more to the point, I never would have gone up to Scotland that third and last time because, although I never could quite understand it at the time (yes, I know, I should have done, but I didn't), Paul's retreat in Scotland was his escape from The Beatles and Beatlemania.

The rights and wrongs of the matter aren't important any more – not to me. It was emotion – his and mine – that led to what happened. Beatlemania and Beatle music are all about emotion, and in 1971 emotions among the group and the fans were mixed and running high.

As the year began I continued to watch and wait outside 7 Cavendish Avenue. I've told you before why I was there, and by now you either understand or you don't. I can't qualify my reasons any more than I have done already.

There were still magic moments to capture. I mean, who would ever imagine Paul McCartney going for a ride on a *bicycle*? But that's what I saw in January when he and his whole family went cycling through the streets of London. On the back of Paul's bike baby Mary was safely and snugly strapped. Heather rode on the back of Linda's cycle. I was totally amazed, for here was a man who had recently been so intent on shunning the public spotlight, but I was touched too by the sight of this portion of an obviously enjoyable family outing. Despite what the fans thought about Paul marrying Linda, here was something that reminded me strongly of my own religious upbringing that had taught me there was nothing more important in this world than the family unit.

But what it also showed me was that out of the four Beatles Paul was, perhaps, the most simplistic. Recently he said, 'I get my pleasures from quite simple things. It's only because I'm "the famous Paul McCartney" people think there's anything unusual about it.'

During his earlier days in St John's Wood he used to take the bus into town. He recalls George once saying to him, 'What are you going on buses for, man? You can get a Ferrari.'

Says Paul, 'Everyone always did think it was a bit nutty, but it's kind of important to me. I like to feel light.'

It's true that Paul did buy a Rolls, but he also had a Mini that he used just as much, if not more than, the Rolls. And it was the idea of a simple life in the country that eventually led him to move right out of London and on to his farm in Scotland.

There was no doubt that now The Beatles – and the fans – were no longer a part of his life. His greatest commitment was to his wife and children, and you couldn't help but admire him for that. But it made us all feel a certain sense of rejection because all The Beatles were still such a large part of our lives, and for me Paul was still someone I wanted to be a friend to.

But by then it was an impossibility. Maybe it always had been, but as he drew his family ever more tightly about him, the barriers that protected him from the outside world became impenetrable. A couple of days after seeing him and his family out cycling, I and another girl stood waiting for him to return to his house, just so we could say 'Hello.' He'd been gone about 45 minutes before he returned.

'Hello Paul,' I said.

He glared at us. 'I've told you two not to come around before,' he retorted.

A simple 'Hello' would have sufficed. That's all we wanted. All we expected. Not to be told off.

Tension over the future of The Beatles continued to soar until, finally, on 19 February, Paul took the other three Beatles to court to dissolve the group legally. Along with some other girls, I decided to go along to the first court session to hear his affidavit read.

We were all a bit anxious about going because we knew he would probably prefer not to see us there, but if this was to be the total and absolute end of our greatest love in the world, we wanted to be present. A reporter for the *Daily Mail*, Celia Haddon, was there and became interested in what I had to say.

After the hearing, Linda announced to the eagerly waiting newspaper reporters that she was expecting another baby in September. The McCartney clan was growing and strengthening while his old 'family' was coming to an end in what Derek Taylor described as a 'horrendous' way. The problem was, The Beatles' business affairs were so complicated with so many fingers in so many Apple pies that it was necessary for Paul literally to take the rest of The Beatles to court to dissolve the partnership.

But there were other matters on the other three Beatles' minds that must have distracted them from the trauma of it all. Ringo had been filming *200 Motels* at Pinewood Studios and on location in London at the beginning of 1971. He played dual roles – that of a character called Larry the Dwarf, and Frank Zappa who was a real-life rock star. Keith Moon of The Who was also in the film. Filming finished in February.

George, that month, was involved in producing a new Badfinger album. A fan called Vicky went Georgewatching at EMI. One day she saw George arrive with Pattie in her red Mercedes. It was an amusing little incident. Pattie had trouble manoeuvring her way into their parking lot, but George, as calm as ever, simply reached over and helped her to turn the wheel just enough to prevent any damage occurring to her car and the others parked close by.

There seemed a deep love between the two. Vicky watched as George got out of the car and waited for Pattie. He put his arm around her and together they went up the steps and into the studio. It was a rare sight to see Pattie down at EMI.

But their marriage wasn't all roses. In fact, things had become strained between them because she wanted to resume her modelling career, and George, who always seemed to think of others, for whatever reasons he had, refused to let her. This led to a number of rows which would, within the next year, lead to a serious rift in the marriage which was a shock and a sadness to all the fans.

In March I left my job in Cavendish Close and secured another at a hospital at the top of Cavendish Avenue, so like it or not Paul still had me for a neighbour. It was a calculated move on my part. But I suppose by this time I should have realized there would never be the same kind of relationship between Paul and any fan that there had once been. But I hadn't learned my lesson. I had to learn the hard way.

During March there was some talk of The Beatles replacing Paul with Klaus Voorman who was a fine musician and a close friend of the group. John Lennon was quick to quash the rumour. The fact was, nobody could have taken Paul's place until he was technically and legally out of the group and for a while John, Ringo and George were appealing against the dissolution of The Beatles' partnership. But by the end of April they had decided to drop their appeal. A receiver and a manager were appointed by the court to look after The Beatles' affairs until the partnership was legally ended.

That was the end of The Beatles.

There was much speculation as to what finally caused the break-up. Many blamed Yoko Ono for taking John's attention away from the group, and to an extent this has to be true. But there had been too many artistic differences between John and Paul, who were after all the main creative force behind The Beatles – which isn't to say that George and Ringo's contributions were any less important.

Anything less than the Fab Four was less than fabulous. For instance, a friend of mine, Renee from The Netherlands, who watched The Beatles in concert in Holland during the European concert tour that Ringo missed through illness, said that Ringo's substitute, Jimmy Nicol, 'did well, but acted rather unBeatleish although he did his best.' A Beatles concert without Ringo singing *I Wanna Be Your Man* (which after all always received the loudest screams) was like a doughnut without the jam – delicious, but you knew something was missing!

It seems to me it all began the day Linda came into Paul's life. Before that day, even when he was with Jane Asher, he poured all his love, dedication and energy into The Beatles and his brainchild, Apple. He inspired the other Beatles, through Apple, to catch the vision of total independence, and through their independence they came to believe they could change the world.

As Derek Taylor told Mike Munn,

We all thought we could change the world. That's what was so unique about the Sixties because people wanted the world to change and thought that was the time to do it. The Beatles, and all of us who were involved with them, thought it could be done through Apple.

We set up the Apple boutique where anybody but anybody could come in, make themselves at home, have a cup of coffee and feel they were among friends.

The Beatles advertised for anyone who wanted to make a film or promote some worthy cause to come to them at Apple and they would give them the money they needed.

Of course, this resulted in The Beatles being besieged with requests that they could never in a million years cope with. It was a noble idea – typical of The Beatles – but

unrealistic in the light of day. Eventually the Apple shop
closed down and all the clothes were given away. And we
stopped trying to change the world.

Well, they didn't stop entirely. They merely stopped doing it
together. They went their separate ways, but John never
ceased trying to bring love and peace to the world, George
found his own peace through his personal beliefs, Ringo
continued making people laugh in films and on TV, and Paul
went on to blow his own pipes of peace on country farms,
proving perhaps that each of us must find his own way. And
each has performed for charity on many occasions.

But the vision of Apple was over, and so too was The
Beatles. Paul's next vision was to settle down and become a
family man, and if divorce should ever be considered a mark
of failure, then to date Paul has been the most successful of
The Beatles, being the only one not to have divorced.

I admire Paul for making his marriage work under the most
difficult of circumstances, and that is why I am sure he
changed so much even to the point of slighting his fans. But he
soon discovered that he still needed the fans when, in May
1971, at a ball he hosted at The Empire Ballroom in London's
Leicester Square, he announced that he would be setting up a
new band called Wings.

In May Celia Haddon of the *Daily Mail* interviewed me and
wrote an article which appeared in the newspaper on 10 May.
Of all the reporters I'd met, she was by far the friendliest and
most sincere. In those days there were always reporters trying
to get information out of the fans – mainly because they
couldn't get it out of The Beatles – but rarely did they look out
for our interests, or The Beatles'. They often made us look
foolish.

A typical example was when two girls, who used to meet
each other outside Paul's house during their lunchbreaks,
were approached by two reporters from the *Kilburn Times*.
The reporters asked the girls if they could take photos of
them. The girls said, 'No.'

Then the reporters asked if they'd give them a story.

'No.'

Unfortunately, the girls allowed themselves to respond to a couple of seemingly innocent questions, and before they knew it a huge article about them appeared in the newspaper which made a complete mockery of the fans. One of the girls involved wrote to the paper asking them to apologize, but her letter was neither published nor answered.

Derek Taylor was himself a reporter for a national daily newspaper before becoming The Beatles' press agent. He was never one of the cruel breed of journalists, and even defied his editor who ordered him to interview The Beatles in 1963 with the intention of writing an article that would tell the world The Beatles were finished. Derek has never said, or written, an unkind word about anyone, and he wasn't about to then. He told Mike Munn,

I was sent up to interview them when they were performing in some far-flung provincial town with the sole purpose of writing a feature that the editor had already decided would say that The Beatles were finished because they'd sold out to their fans by agreeing to appear on the Palladium show. I think his idea was that by doing the Palladium they were going to play to an audience that was not really theirs. It was the kind of show that the likes of Matt Monroe and Nina and Frederick appeared on, not long-haired rock stars.

So I went along and saw their concert and I thought they were fabulous and so likeable. I mean, it was impossible not to like them, and so when I went backstage to meet them I'd already decided I wasn't going to write the story my editor wanted.

You couldn't help but love them. Even John who could be so cynical. He came in, saw me and said, 'Who's this?'

Someone said I'd come to interview them for an important national newspaper, and he just said 'Oh' and turned around and went out again. But that *was* John. And you loved him for it.

They were really just ordinary people. Four boys having a good time who never really wanted to be as famous as they became. When they were asked a question by any reporters and they didn't know the answer, they'd say 'I don't know.' They are the only famous people I know of who ever said that because normally in an interview whoever it is being interviewed always comes up with some answer, even if they don't know what they're talking about. But The Beatles were honest in everything. So how could I write a story saying they'd sold out, that they were finished? I contacted my editor and told him with some apprehension that The Beatles were here to stay and that was to be my story.

As it happened, the Palladium show wasn't the end, but really the beginning.

But now it really was the end – for me, it was the end of everything.

Everyone said 'Don't go back to Campbeltown.' But Paul was there, and I was stuck in London and missing him. I was debating whether or not I should make a third visit to his farm that June of 1971. I knew deep-down that Paul would not appreciate my going up to see him, but I felt that it couldn't hurt if I was simply to remain at an unintrusive distance and maybe somehow gain his tolerance and even trust – or perhaps more to the point, Linda's trust. There was no reason, as far as I could see, why I should be considered some kind of threat.

I thought it over for some time and decided it was worth giving it a try. The thing was, I had made a real sacrifice for the most important thing in my life, leaving behind my family and friends, my secure Mormon home in Salt Lake City, all the people I'd known all my life – all just to get as close to The Beatles, and Paul in particular, as I could. So I decided now was the time to make another sacrifice; I gave up my job at the hospital so I could spend all the time I needed in Scotland.

My friends were panic-stricken. They all warned me not to go. But I felt it was now or never, and besides, I was fed up with my job and this seemed as good a time as ever to quit and take a well-needed break. This was to be a holiday that I hoped would be the best vacation of my life.

It proved to be the worst. It was also the biggest mistake of my life.

I suppose at that time of my life I felt so strongly that I could somehow, after all I'd been through, after all the love I'd tried to show, become a real friend to Paul. But what I didn't appreciate then was that Paul had made the kind of life he wanted with the only people he wanted, and that excluded not just me but also the people he'd been closer to than anyone – The Beatles. After all the trauma of the concert tours, the heady and crazy highs of fame and fortune, the phenomenon of Beatlemania, and the noisy and high-speed trappings of urban life, he had found what he wanted in Scotland.

John Lennon had spent part of his early years in Scotland, and it was his descriptions of the Highlands and the fields and the valleys and the lakes that inspired Paul to go and take a look for himself.

He had been living in urban surroundings for most of his life – certainly all his adult life. Then one day he got to thinking that all childhood had gone, and he remembered as a small boy lying in a field and smelling the grass and making daisy chains. He looked about his St John's Wood surroundings and thought that it was all gone.

'Then,' he says, 'I realized it was *me* who had gone. It was all still there.'

When he married Linda he started going back up to Scotland with more frequency. Then, when the children came along, he and Linda decided to move right out of London for the sake of their children.

'Linda and I both thought it would be nice to try to bring the kids up a little bit like our lives were when we were kids,' he says, 'so they can go out on their bikes, play with their friends in the road, have neighbours to talk to, go into village shops and all that – a more normal way to grow up.

'The only way to do that these days is to be in the country. You'll still find it all there; just like it was 50 years ago.'

On his farm in Campbeltown, his life was totally different from the way it had been in London. It was how he wanted it – not having to live behind high walls and big black gates, and having hordes of fans constantly waiting outside his house all day and all night. I realize now we had all helped to make Paul feel trapped – not at first, though, because he enjoyed the adulation and attention. But when he settled down into a would-be real family life, he realized he had to escape all that. It was never so bad for the other Beatles – they all lived outside London. But, after all, Paul was the one to choose to live in the middle of London and he was quite happy to handle the fans in his own way.

He recalls,

> At the height of The Beatles, I once walked into one of the Odeon cinemas on the outskirts of London. This crowd of 30 girls came running towards me screaming, but I had this method I've always clung to.
>
> I said, 'Right, what do you want? Hey, hey, you stop that. Now, do you want an autograph? Look, if you stop, I'll do it. Be cool. Good.'
>
> And we used to stand and talk and that was great. I see myself in an elder brother kind of role.

Of course, elder brother sometimes got mad, and when he felt the need to break away from that role and everything that was associated with The Beatles, he got madder than ever and more often. Now, free of The Beatles, and hardly on speaking terms with any of them for the time being, he set out to make a whole new way of life for himself and his family.

The last thing he wanted, so far away from all he'd escaped from, was me turning up on his farm. Like I said, if I knew then what I know now – but that's life. It's all about making mistakes and learning by them – and both Paul and I made mistakes.

On 30 June I turned up at Mr McDougal's farm with blood pouring from my nose and a huge bruise growing on my hand. I was shaking and bewildered. He and his wife took me in and asked how I'd got in such a state.

I told them that Paul had punched me. They cleaned me up and told me that I must report the incident to the police.

Confused and still in shock, I did as they said and made my long way back into the village to the police station. I was asked to make a statement which they would send to the Procurator Fiscal who would decide if any charges should be brought against Paul. I don't recall word for word what the report said but my allegation against Paul went something along these lines.

I told the police how I'd arrived in Campbeltown five days ago and booked into a boarding house, hoping to catch a glimpse of Paul and his family on their shopping trips into the town's main street. On the fifth day I decided to walk up to Paul's farm in the hope of catching sight of him there. I got as far as Mr McDougal's farm and, exhausted from the long trek, I sat down.

I wasn't even on Paul's property. I explained to the police how Paul and Linda drove up to me in a jeep. Linda was shouting at me as they pulled up. Then I told them that Paul jumped out, came over to me and began hitting me. I was so shocked, I had no real sense of how many times he hit me but I received at least two knocks because my nose began to bleed and as the bruise later came up on my hand I realized I must have received that in trying to protect myself, although all the details were so hazy. I don't even recall a word he said to me. I told the police that only when he stopped hitting me did I actually realize what had just happened.

Well, that's what I told the police, and before I knew it reporters from everywhere were descending on me. I can only assume that someone at the police station had tipped them off because I certainly never told anyone other than the police and the McDougals. And I don't believe the McDougals would have called the newspapers.

Well, whoever called them, they certainly thought that it would make a great story if they took me up to Paul's farm and got him to apologize. I was still in a daze and fell for their sympathetic talk. But that's all it was – talk. They stood with their little tape recorders and notebooks and pens ready to record for posterity his every word. They didn't really care what he said, so long as he said something to give them more meat to what was already tomorrow's headlines.

They were forcing Paul into an impossible situation. What could he say? Did they really expect him to incriminate himself in tomorrow's national newspapers? Well, of course they didn't expect that at all, and they went happily away with his denial of the episode, and I was left to feel like a fool and a liar.

According to the *Daily Express*, Paul admitted he had been annoyed at seeing me in a field overlooking his field and had told me to go away. He told the *Daily Mail*, 'I moved here for peace and quiet, not to have cranks and sightseers around. If I didn't try to stop girls invading the privacy of my home here, I'd never get rid of them.'

I must admit, if he had apologized I would have immediately dropped the charges, but at the time it seemed to me that I'd been the victim and I was angry and hurt. But I now realize that Paul was as much the victim, mainly thanks to the newspaper reporters. I had never intended to put Paul on the spot like that; I was manoeuvred into doing it, and I regret it now. I knew then that Paul would never trust me and I'd be nothing more to him than another troublesome fan – more troublesome than all the others. And that was the last thing on my mind – causing him trouble.

I'd never felt so miserable in my life. And there was no way now I could prevent the rest of the world from hearing about it.

Two of my friends later told me that they were sitting on an underground train in London and happened to glance over at somebody else's newspaper and were shocked to see my picture with the story about the incident. Another girl I knew from Newcastle was woken up by her mother who'd heard the news on early morning radio. When her mother told her they'd given out my name on the air, my friend almost fell out of bed with horror.

My sister Genevieve wrote from Salt Lake City and said that she first heard about it on the news on television. Another girl wrote and told me she saw an article about the allegations in an Indianapolis newspaper. Then an article appeared about me in the *Salt Lake Tribune* and even the Mormon newspaper, the *Desert News*, printed a story.

Back in Campbeltown, I stayed away from Paul's farm and made sure I avoided the main street of the village in case I should bump into him there. I spent much of my time after the incident sitting by the water-front, thinking long and hard about what had happened. Fortunately, I hadn't sustained any serious physical harm – my bruised hand had been X-rayed and was thankfully not broken as the doctor had at

first feared – and for several days I was stranded in Campbeltown as I had no money to pay for the return fare to London. I
had used up all I had paying for the bed and breakfast
lodgings. Friends in London sent me the fare to get home.

Then, as the *Daily Mail* (one of the few newspapers to
publish a favourable report on me) put it,

> Beatles' fan Carolyn Mitchell took a last look yesterday at
> the long, winding road that leads to Paul McCartney's
> remote hideaway farm in Scotland.
> Then she left for home in St John's Wood, London.
> Carolyn, 24, who left her parent's [sic] home in Salt
> Lake City, Utah, two years ago to go 'Beatle chasing'
> around Britain said, 'I won't be back here.'

John Lennon was in his element and looking great as he sat
with Yoko in the Claude Gill bookshop in Oxford Street,
where they were signing paperback copies of Yoko's book
Grapefruit.

I was there with my friend Vicky who kept buying copies of
the book (five in all) so she could keep going up to the front to
get John and Yoko to sign all five copies. There was such a
crush by enthusiastic fans Vicky said she almost got killed in
the process, but I had to agree with her that the adulation and
respect everyone had for John and Yoko was 'very heart
warming'. John looked really well and happy, and he said that
a book signing was 'something different'.

He was so calm and didn't seem at all bothered by the still
evident Beatlemania that ensued, although there was nothing
like the pandemonium that he and the other Beatles came to
hate so much.

Then, among all those people, he recognized me and gave
me a wave which really made my day. To think that he should
remember *me*. Also, he must have known about my allegation against Paul (it remained an 'allegation' since no
charges were ever brought against Paul, which, in hindsight,
was probably for the best as any ensuing court case would just
have made things worse), but his smile and wave to me proved
that he for one didn't believe I was a troublesome fan.

At the end of the signing, he and Yoko went out of the back

door of the shop, smiling and very happy, and doing a funny little dance. He really was an amazing man, to be so calm and at peace after all the problems he and Yoko had faced in the preceding months. In April, while in Majorca, the couple were accused of kidnapping Yoko's seven-year-old daughter, Kyoko. It was Yoko's ex-husband, Anthony Cox, who made the accusation, and John and Yoko were arrested and taken to the police station with poor little Kyoko lovingly carried in John's arms. The couple had been trying for two years to get custody of the child.

In June they flew to New York in search of Kyoko who was being kept hidden by Cox, and although they continued to try and gain custody, they finally lost the battle.

A month later here were both John and Yoko, looking for all the world like they didn't have a care in the world. Their public faces must have belied the inner anxiety that Yoko in particular must have been suffering.

Outside the bookstore, a girl came up to John and handed him a grapefruit to sign. (Grapefruits had been handed out to everyone in the shop.) John said, 'I can't sign it with the pen I've got.'

The girl said, 'Well, try it anyway,' so he did. He signed a lot more autographs before being whisked away in his car.

A month later there was further evidence that Beatlemania hadn't completely died with The Beatles, when George Harrison staged a charity benefit at the New York Madison Square Garden for the Bangladesh people. Kris Martell and her friend Sarah went to the evening performance which was filmed and released in cinemas as *Concert For Bangladesh*. The impressive line-up of artistes included Ringo, Eric Clapton, Leon Russell, Billy Preston and Bob Dylan among others.

Kris told me that the whole block surrounding Madison Square was packed with people. Hundreds of fans had slept at Pen Station the previous night waiting for the afternoon performance to begin.

She said that the evening concert she went to was almost like a Beatle concert. The show began in pitch darkness. Then all of a sudden a spotlight came on and onto the stage walked George Harrison. He was applauded for about five minutes non-stop. The enthusiasm and love were still there among the fans, but, unlike the old days of Beatlemania, there was no screaming.

Pattie Harrison and Maureen Starr sat together in the front row with the photographers. Also in the audience were Yoko's sister and George's father.

At the end of the concert Eric Clapton showed his appreciation for George and the whole band applauded him. He and Ringo hugged each other warmly. There were tears and smiles and waves. Kris said it was more emotional than any Beatle concert that she'd seen.

So, John, George and Ringo were well in their own elements away from The Beatles. But what about Paul? Well, he was in the process of setting up his new band, Wings, but the adverse publicity over the Campbeltown incident couldn't have helped, and he obviously wouldn't have thanked me for that. I knew that I had to face him, if only just the once, to discover just what his attitude to me would be. I was nervous – scared to death – but when he came back to London, I was there waiting for him.

I said, 'Do you want me to go?'

I might have expected him to explode and shout 'Yes, and don't ever come back.' But he really looked quite sorry and he replied, 'You don't have to go.'

I felt it was his way of saying sorry, and that made me feel much better.

The publicity hadn't only affected Paul. It hit me hard too because when I went back to the employment agency, which had found me my previous jobs, they told me they couldn't help me further as the Campbeltown incident would make bad publicity for them also.

Around 13 September I went to King's College Hospital when Paul's daughter, Stella, was born. Soon after that I stopped going to Cavendish Avenue altogether.

It was inevitable that I wouldn't spend all my life watching after The Beatles. I'm sure it was what happened in Scotland which finally put me off and I know my friends were very surprised when I said I wasn't going to Cavendish Avenue any more, because they knew how crazy I was about Paul McCartney. I took my feelings for him so seriously, for such a long time. That's the way I am. When I feel strongly about someone or something, all of my energies go so deeply. I am a very emotional person, but despite all the emotion I felt for Paul, after the Scotland incident the penny finally dropped that I'd come to a dead end.

But I never stopped being a fan – and I never stopped loving The Beatles, as a group or as individuals.

CHAPTER TWELVE

Get Back? ('It's All Over')

A FRIEND WENT to see Wings at Frankfurt Offenbach City
Halle on 19 July 1972, during the band's first European tour.
She told me,

> There was no introduction for Wings. They just went on
> stage when the curtain went up and everyone in the audi-
> ence clapped and cheered. Paul looked relieved and
> smiled. He still stood in exactly the same way at the
> microphone and looked like he did in 1964. He still teased
> the microphone. He seemed to concentrate more on
> playing bass.
>
> Paul and Denny Laine sang harmony and sounded fan-
> tastic. Paul looked really happy to be on stage and seemed
> to be at home after the first song. He asked how many
> Americans were in the audience and seemed surprised
> when 80 per cent of the audience clapped.
>
> But there were no screams or hysterical scenes.

Wings became a very important part of Paul's life. He still
needed to have a working band, but it was never as dominant
in his life as The Beatles had been. It was also a very different
format from the Fabulous Four because now his band consisted of five members, including Linda, and that spoiled it for
me from the start. She had never accepted the fans and there
were always arguments between her and us. When she joined
Wings, that was too much for me.

I went to quite a lot of Wings concerts, but I only went to
see Paul. I never was a Wings fan. But it was rewarding to see
him perform live on stage, especially as I'd never seen The
Beatles as a live working group. He accomplished so much
with his new group, even though he seemed unsure of their
potential when they first began. After all, how do you follow
The Beatles?

To try them out for size, he took them on the road early in 1972 and gave some unannounced concerts. For instance, he'd turn up at universities and say, 'How'd you like Paul McCartney and his new band to play here?'

By June Wings had had its first hit with *Mary Had A Little Lamb* before hitting the concert trail in Europe. At that time Paul wasn't in touch with the other Beatles. They just refused to talk to him, but he had his own band to worry about now. He also had bigger worries. In August he, Linda and their drummer Denny Seiwell were arrested in Sweden on drugs charges.

It happened during a concert when police searched their dressing rooms at the Gothenberg Scandinavian Halle, as well as the band's psychedelicly designed London bus. Over 3,500 fans in the audience clapped and cheered, waiting for the band to appear as police whisked the group off to the police station with a packet containing seven ounces of cannabis they'd found.

After several hours of interrogation Paul, Linda and Denny admitted they had had the cannabis especially sent over from England for their use. They were fined a total of £800. It wasn't the last time Paul and Linda were busted on drugs charges as they continued to use cannabis, claiming it was a lot less harmful than cigarettes or alcohol.

By 1973 Paul had proved that he was a star in his own right and ATV filmed a TV special, *James Paul McCartney*. He also gave a charity concert at the London Hard Rock Café which was filmed and released in cinemas in March.

Wings continued to tour and at the end of their British tour in 1973 Paul hosted a party in May at the Café Royal in London. Here he displayed his musical dexterity by giving a performance in which he alternated between playing piano, drums and lead guitar. Among the guests who performed with him was Elton John. One of the greatest pop stars of the Sixties was now in the company of the new glam-rock stars of the Seventies, proving he could compete with the best of them as well as still be one of them, which, considering the history of most rock and pop stars, was quite a feat. That Paul McCartney is still a major force in today's music scene isn't something you can put down to mere luck or perseverance.

What Paul has is an amazing and enduring mixture of star quality and immeasureable musical ability.

As his success with Wings grew, the likelihood of a Beatles reunion became less probable. Following a phenomenal concert by Wings at Madison Square Garden during their American tour of 1976, Paul said, 'At last I'm happy. This is how I want to live. This is my destiny. Don't talk to me about a Beatles' reunion. Who needs it?'

Paul McCartney, for one, had no intention of getting back with John, George and Ringo. And, by and large, the other three Beatles certainly didn't want to get together with him again, and even socially they were still out of touch with him. But rumours that The Beatles were to reunite kept surfacing. That was an event every fan longed for.

There were, however, times when The Beatles, or rather the ex-Beatles, did unite, if only through the lawyers. For instance, in 1977 they and Apple took out an injunction against the release of The Beatles' live double-album *Live At The Star Club, Hamburg 1962*. Counsel for the Beatles and the Apple organization said that their appeal was based on the fact that the recordings were of poor quality.

But in London's High Court, Vice-Chancellor Sir Robert Megarry decided not to grant the injunction. He said that two members of the group had, two years earlier, been offered the tapes for around £10,000 but had refused them.

As far as the fans were concerned, any new Beatles record was something we wanted. It seems ironic that this was a time when we, the fans, would have preferred The Beatles not to have agreed on something. The only thing that we wanted them to agree on was performing together again.

Certainly, as far as Paul was concerned, that could never happen – at least, not while Wings were still going strong. Also, now that his wife was a part of his musical life, his family life was something which went with him everywhere. It was, I suppose, a case of home is where the heart is.

His family increased on 12 September 1977, when Linda gave birth to their first son, James. This was also the year Paul released *Mull Of Kintyre*, which went on to break just about every record in music history. Then, in 1979, his stature as a musician was further enhanced when the *Guinness Book of*

Records named him the most successful composer of all time. He had received 42 gold discs with The Beatles, 17 with Wings and one with Billy Preston, totalling 60 gold discs in all. His estimated record sales totalled one hundred million albums and one hundred million singles, making him the most successful recording artist in the world. To honour him as such Norris McWhirter, editor of the *Guinness Book of Records*, presented him with a unique disc made of rhodium, a metal twice as valuable as platinum.

On 16 January 1980 Paul was again arrested on drugs charges, this time in Tokyo. While he was going through customs, officials found plastic bags containing eight ounces of marijuana in his suitcase. Wings had come to Japan for an 11 date concert tour, but now Paul faced the possibility of spending the next five years in a Japanese prison. He was lucky to get off lightly with just a few days in jail and deportation.

Speculation was still rife that The Beatles would get together again. All that ended at the end of 1980. John Lennon was murdered in cold blood.

The winter of 1972 was the time of the great power cuts in the UK. For everyone they were an intolerable nuisance, but for the fans they very nearly put an end to the possibility of The Beatles ever reuniting, because in February George Harrison crashed his car into a roundabout that was steeped in darkness because the street lights were off. Pattie was dragged unconscious from the wreck. George, mercifully, emerged with nothing more than severe cuts to his face.

By May they were fully recovered and went to the Cannes Film Festival with Ringo and Maureen for a screening of *Concert For Bangladesh*. The break-up of The Beatles had not harmed the friendships of John, George and Ringo. Oddly enough, though, none of The Beatles attended the London *première* of the film in July which was a huge disappointment to all us fans who gathered outside the Rialto cinema in the hope of seeing them. It was all a far cry from the days of *A Hard Day's Night* when police had to hold back the milling, screaming thousands who thronged to see The Beatles arrive for the *première*.

In 1974 George made his independence even stronger by breaking away from the Apple label and signing an exclusive deal with A&M Records to form his own label which he called Dark Horse Records. Shortly after that his marriage broke up when he began dating Kathy Simmonds, ex-girlfriend of Rod Stewart.

Still, the question on everybody's lips was, 'Will The Beatles get back together?'

At a press conference in October, George answered that question. He said,

It's a very slim possibility at the moment. Everybody's enjoying being individual. I mean, we were boxed up together for ten years, and personally I'm enjoying playing with the band I've got on tour.

I realize The Beatles did fill a space in the Sixties, and all the people who The Beatles meant something to have all grown up. It's like anything; if you grow up with something you get attached to it. One of the problems in our lives is that we get attached to things. I can understand that The Beatles did nice things and it's appreciated that people still like them.

The problem comes when they want to live in the past, when they want to hold on to something. People are afraid of change.

The point is that it's all fantasy, the idea of putting The Beatles together again. If we ever do that, the reason will be that we're all broke. There's more chance that we'll do it because we're broke than because . . . ! And even then, to play with The Beatles . . . ! I mean, I'd rather have Willie Weeks (his bass guitarist) on bass than Paul McCartney. That's the truth, with all due respect to Paul. The Beatles was like being in a box. We got to that point. It's taken me years to be able to play with other musicians. Because we were so isolated it became very difficult playing the same tunes, day in, day out.

Since I made *All Things Must Pass*, it's so nice for me to be able to play with other musicians and having played with other musicians, I don't think The Beatles were that good. I think they're fine, you know.

Ringo's got the best back beat I ever heard. He hates drum solos. Paul is a fine bass player. He's a bit overpowering at times. John's gone through all his scene but he feels like me; he's come back around. We're all at that point. I mean, to tell you the truth, I'd join a band with John Lennon any day, but I couldn't join a band with Paul McCartney, but it's nothing personal. It's just from a musical point of view.

The biggest break in my career was getting into The Beatles. The biggest break in retrospect since then was getting out of them.

George did his first solo American tour, and (just my luck) even played the Salt Lake City Palace; if only The Beatles had done that all those years ago!

While in the United States he began dating his secretary Olivia Arias. Before returning to England to live with Olivia in his castle in Henley, he held a party at the Hippopotamus night club in New York to celebrate his Dark Horse Tour, and among his guests were John and Yoko.

Despite his very serious, sober approach to life, George was a great fan of the Monty Python comedy team, and in 1976 he made a surprise appearance at the New York City Centre by accepting an invitation to leave the audience and join the Monty Python team on stage where they were performing. He donned a Royal Canadian Mounted Police uniform and joined them in the lumberjack sketch. The lumberjack song was a favourite of his and he had used it during his tour to introduce each show.

His meeting the Monty Python team was something of a turning point for George.

Trouble became commonplace that year for him. He became ill with food poisoning in London and his illness turned into hepatitis. During his illness A&M Records were involved in a law suit with Dark Horse Records because, said A&M, George had failed to fulfil their contract. George had thought all their problems were in the process of being sorted out in various meetings until A&M suddenly sued him for £6 million.

His legal problems weren't over even then. He was successfully sued for plagiarism of *He's So Fine* which, it was said, he based his hit single *My Sweet Lord* on. He had to pay a fortune in costs. It was unfair – there are a lot of songs around that sound familiar and most of the time nobody says anything. It seems that as soon as a Beatle does such a thing, the whole matter is blown out of proportion.

In 1977 George and Pattie divorced. It was so hard to believe such a thing could happen to them, of all people.

It's incredible to think that with so much bad luck on his side, he could maintain his sense of humour. When Eric Idle (of the Monty Python team) produced a TV special which was a direct spoof on the lives of The Beatles (only in this called The Rutles), entitled *All You Need Is Cash*, George did a cameo playing a TV reporter. It was clever and hilarious – George was one Beatle unafraid of sending up the old Fab Four image.

August 1978 was a happy time for him. His girlfriend, Olivia, gave birth to their son and named him Dhani. George was present at the birth. With the divorce from Pattie now final and with a son to nurture, George secretly married Olivia in a registry office just 200 yards from their Henley home. The only wedding guests were Olivia's parents and the witnesses. (George's father had sadly passed away in May.)

George became ever more involved with his favourite comedy team in 1979 when he invested around £2 million in *Monty Python's Life Of Brian*. The original backers had pulled out because of the growing controversy over the nature of the film, which was said to be a spoof on the life of Jesus Christ. In fact, the film actually portrayed Christ, albeit briefly, as Himself while the action was centred on a completely different character called Brian. George even played a cameo in one scene. To raise the money he had mortgaged his house, but the film was so successful he earned a fortune from it which prompted him to turn his hand to film-making through his own company, Handmade Films. He has since become something of an Eighties mini-movie mogul.

He also turned his hand to writing a book, *I Me Mine*, which was published during the summer of 1980 at the staggering price of £148.00. He described his book as 'The small change

of a short lifetime and a little ego detour . . . I have suffered
for this book. Now it's your turn.'

I'm afraid I didn't suffer. I never bought it. At that price, I
wonder who did!

Long before George ever had an inclination to dabble in
movie-making, Ringo Starr had set up a film department at
Apple, and in 1972 he put together *Born To Boogie* featuring
Mark Bolan and T Rex. Ringo didn't miss the opportunity of
also appearing in the film. His acting career was strengthened
in 1973 when he co-starred with David Essex in *That'll Be The
Day*, an affectionate look at the fifties with Ringo playing a
teddy boy.

He still had an interest in the music world as well, and in
1974 he followed George's example by setting up his own
label, Ring O'Records. But films were taking precedence in
his life. In 1974 he produced *Son Of Dracula*, a rock/horror
picture starring Harry Nilsson, with Ringo in the part of
Merlin the Magician!

Ringo invested $80,000 in the movie which was partly shot
in Hampstead. I went along there one day and saw a little of
the filming. Ringo was in great form and looked decidedly
happy on a film set – just as happy, if not happier, than he'd
ever been behind a set of drums.

The film *premièred* in Atlanta, Georgia and was never
heard of again. As a film producer, Ringo was a lot less
successful than he was just being an actor.

His next picture was *Lisztomania* for Ken Russell, and he
appeared on stage in The Who's rock opera *Tommy*.

By this time Ringo's marriage was on the rocks and
Maureen filed for divorce, charging Ringo with adultery
and naming a Nancy Andrews as the other woman.

Ringo had also become something of a TV personality by
this time – more so than any of the other Beatles – and he
often guest-starred on other people's shows. His Teddy bear
image and zany personality made him a favourite, especially
in America, but when it came to picking film roles, it was all
too often a hit and miss affair. At the beginning of 1977 he was
busy filming *Sextette* with Mae West. It was a disaster and
hardly saw the light of day. But he was very much at home in

the part of a European film director and ex-husband of Mae West, which allowed him to indulge in some crazy antics.

In 1978 he starred in a 60-minute TV special simply called *Ringo*, although it was loosely based on *The Prince And The Pauper*. It co-starred Angie Dickinson, Vincent Price and Carrie Fisher. But it was never screened outside the United States.

Again his health let him down early in 1979 and he was rushed to hospital suffering from long-term after-effects of peritonitis which he had had when he was six. He very nearly died. To save his life doctors in Monte Carlo removed five feet of his intestines. He said after, 'I would have died if they hadn't done it. But it still blows me away to think of all they have taken out of me.'

Fully recovered some months later, he appeared live on *The Jerry Lewis Labor Day Telethon*. His TV appearances were, by now, far more successful than his movie roles. Early in 1980 he went to Mexico to make the movie *Caveman*, a so-called comedy set in pre-historic times. It was another disaster, but one good thing came out of it. He fell in love with his leading lady, the beautiful Barbara Bach who'd previously made her name in the James Bond film *The Spy Who Loved Me*.

In May of that year the two were involved in a serious car crash in South London. Five minutes after the crash Ringo managed to get to his feet. He found a packet of cigarettes from the wreck. He lit two and gave one to Barbara who was in severe shock. The Beatles have certainly been relatively lucky whenever one of them has been involved in a car crash. First it was John Lennon, then George Harrison, and this time it was Ringo. Ringo seems to have stared death in the face on numerous occasions but has always emerged as perky and as personable as ever.

But death did come to a Beatle that year, wastefully ending a most precious life, along with all our hopes of seeing The Beatles get back.

In 1972, while Paul was still preparing to take Wings on the road, John and Yoko were living in New York and facing deportation. The American authorities were still refusing him a permanent visa. They said it was because John and Yoko had been charged with a drugs offence. But in time John became convinced there was more to it than that.

Friends that I'd made in London and fellow-fans who used to write to me from America still corresponded, and often they would write and tell me that they'd met John in New York and that he was always extremely friendly to them.

That spring, John and Yoko joined thousands of demonstrators in Duffy Square to protest against America's involvement in the Vietnam war. John spoke to the crowd and led the marchers in a chorus of *Give Peace A Chance*.

Pop's oddest couple (which was how the world – not us – saw them) appeared with regularity on various TV chat shows, in which John usually put forward his views on how peace should be accomplished throughout the world. One politician who appeared on a show with him argued the point and even became quite abusive towards John and Yoko. It couldn't have helped the government's insistence that their only reservation about giving John and Yoko visas was because of their drugs offence. The Lennons were becoming convinced that there was a political plot against them and that they were being followed by government agents. The government denied this. Years later, released government documents proved John was correct.

For two such so-called undesirable people, John and Yoko were amazingly generous. In August 1972 they gave two concerts, with all the money going to establish small community residential facilities for the mentally retarded. The following month, they performed live on *The Jerry Lewis Telethon For Muscular Dystrophy*. And these were the kind of people American authorities wanted out of the country!

On 23 March 1973 Judge Ira Fieldsteel of New York ordered John to leave the United States within 60 days or face deportation. John appealed against the decision to the Board of Immigration Appeals in Washington.

The following month Yoko finally won custody of Kyoko but her joy was short lived as her ex-husband Tony Cox suddenly disappeared with Kyoko.

The pressure that was heaped upon them became too much and in October John and Yoko went their separate ways. For a while John seemed to resemble the angry young man who had formed The Quarrymen so many years earlier. A photographer, Brenda Parkins, filed a complaint against John, claiming he hit her while she was taking pictures of him in March 1974. Her charges were dropped so they wouldn't interfere with John's pending immigration action and a settlement was reached out of court.

Then, just a few weeks later, John was thrown out of the Troubador Club in Los Angeles after heckling the Smothers Brothers and then hitting a man who tried to calm him down.

He was again ordered to leave America within 60 days from 17 July and he lodged a further appeal. During August he appeared in the Federal Courts and claimed that the Nixon Administration was trying to have him deported, not because of the drugs offence, but because they believed he was one of the organizers of an anti-war demonstration which was to have been held at the Republican Convention in Miami in 1972. The government again denied this and the Board of Immigration Appeals ordered John to leave the United States voluntarily by 8 September. He lodged another appeal.

He still showed some interest in Beatle nostalgia by turning up at a trial performance of a brand new show called *Sgt Pepper's Lonely Hearts Club Band On The Road* at Greenwich Village. It was based on The Beatles' *Sgt Pepper* album and included 28 Beatles songs in all. The cast was somewhat overawed to meet John Lennon in person and the producers were pleased and relieved to find that John approved of the way the songs worked in the context of the show. Throughout the trial performance John laughed and sang along with the cast and occasionally called out cues when actors forgot their lines.

By this time John, like the other Beatles, was always being asked if The Beatles would reunite. He seemed as determined as the other three that this would never happen, but he did concede to being a Beatles fan, admitting that he enjoyed listening to Beatles records.

At the very beginning of 1975 the US District Court Judge, Richard Owen, ruled in favour of John and his lawyers, permitting them access to the immigration files under certain conditions. Once these were examined John filed suit in

Manhattan Federal Court against former Attorney General John Mitchell, former attorney Richard Kleindienst and other government officials, charging that the deportation actions directed against him were improper. By now John and Yoko were back together again and she was expecting his baby, so a temporary non-priority status was granted to John so he wouldn't have to leave America before the baby was born.

Then, in October, the US Court of Appeals overturned the deportation order against John, saying that the British law under which John had been convicted of drugs offences was unjust by US standards and therefore he had been denied due process. The court decided that John's drug conviction was not a good enough reason for a deportation order against him.

Two days later, on 9 October, John's thirty-fifth birthday, Yoko gave birth to Sean Ono Lennon. Almost a year later, John's application to remain in the United States as a permanent resident was formally approved and he was given his long sought-after green visa card.

John went into semi-retirement, wanting to devote his time to bringing up Sean in their New York apartment. He became a 'house-husband' while Yoko ran their business affairs. Each of them was successful in their respective tasks. Then, towards the end of 1980, John returned to the recording studio to work with Yoko on a brand new album, *Double Fantasy*.

By now much of the bitterness of the break-up of The Beatles had vanished and occasionally John and Paul, though not going out of their way to make friends, refrained from slighting each other publicly and privately. The news that John was back at work again fuelled speculation that the time was coming when The Beatles would reunite.

In September John was quick to quash any such rumours.

I was always waiting for a reason to get out of The Beatles from the day I filmed *How I Won The War*. I just didn't have the guts to do it.

The seed was planted when The Beatles stopped touring and I couldn't deal with not going on stage. But I was too frightened to step out of the palace. That's what killed

Presley. Whatever made The Beatles, The Beatles also made the Sixties.

Anybody who thinks that if John and Paul got together with George and Ringo The Beatles would exist, is out of their skulls. The Beatles gave everything they had to give, and more. The four guys who used to be that group can never be that group again, even if they wanted to be.

What if Paul and I got together? It would be boring. Whether George and Ringo joined in would be irrelevant because Paul and I created the music, okay? But going back to The Beatles would be like going back to school. I was never one for reunions. It's all over.

Three months after he made that statement I saw the headline JOHN LENNON SHOT DEAD on the front of the London *Evening Standard* on 9 December 1980. I hadn't put the radio on that morning so I'd no idea what had happened until I saw that horrendous headline. I just couldn't take it in. It was like a nightmare to think such a thing could happen.

It had happened that morning in New York at four o'clock. John and Yoko were returning to their co-operative apartment building, The Dakota, on Manhattan's Upper West Side, when a so-called fan, Mark Chapman who'd earlier obtained John's autograph, pulled out a .38 calibre hand gun and shot John five times.

John dragged himself up six steps to a small glass booth in the courtyard of the building, moaning, 'I'm shot. I'm shot.'

The doorman gazed up at Chapman and asked, 'Do you know what you just did?'

'I just shot John Lennon,' replied Chapman as he threw down his gun.

John died on the way to hospital.

Tributes poured in from all quarters of the globe.

'We are all terribly upset by John's sudden and tragic death,' said Cynthia Lennon. 'I have always held John in the deepest regard since our divorce and encouraged the relationship between him and Julian.'

John's Aunt Mimi said, 'I still can't believe it. I keep saying to myself "He'll be over soon." He seemed happier now than he had been for a long time. I remember him as the little boy who was happy from morning to night and would sing himself to sleep. We did not have any children of our own. He was our son. He brought greater happiness to myself and my husband George that anyone could bring.'

President Jimmy Carter, successor to John's persecutor Nixon, said, 'John Lennon helped to create the music and spirit of our time. In the songs he composed he leaves an extraordinary and permanent legacy. I know I speak for millions of Americans when I say I am saddened by his death and the senseless manner of it.'

Cilla Black said, 'It's one of the world's greatest tragedies.'

Mick Jagger told reporters, 'I'm absolutely stunned. I knew and liked the man for 18 years. But I don't want to make a casual remark about him now at such an awful moment for his family and his millions of fans and friends.'

But what everyone wanted to know especially was what the surviving Beatles had to say. A spokesman for Ringo said 'He's very shocked. He doesn't want to speak.'

George composed himself enough to say, 'After all we went through together, I still have the greatest love and respect for him. I am shocked and stunned. To rob life is the greatest robbery in life.'

Paul was far too overwhelmed by the tragedy to give reporters an immediate tribute to John. 'I can't take it in at the moment,' he told them.

Later he remarked, 'John was a great man. His death is a bitter, cruel blow. I loved the man. He will be sadly missed by the whole world. John will be remembered for his contribution to art, music and world peace. I can't tell you how much it hurts to lose him.'

In the weeks, months and years that have followed John's death his fans and admirers have virtually raised his status to that of sainthood. But what really counted was the estimation that the rest of the world now held him in. There were those who still scoffed, but there were also many more who had come to recognize that John Lennon was not only an eminently creative musician but also a fine and decent human being.

Perhaps, for me, the saddest thing of all is to have to say that it was a Beatle fan who killed John. I can remember hearing John say that the greatest threat to The Beatles was from the fans. I know that no fan in his or her right mind would ever have wanted to cause the death of a Beatle. It's so painfully ironic that after all the hysteria of Beatlemania had died down, people like myself were more able to meet and talk to The Beatles, and it was that very privilege which allowed Mark Chapman to get close enough to do what he did.

But Mark Chapman didn't just kill John Lennon. He succeeded in killing The Beatles altogether, because now there never could be a reunion. Whether or not that would ever have happened we will never know. Derek Taylor thinks that it's possible, but as he said, 'that's almost too painful to contemplate.'

After The Beatles split, and even long after the death of John Lennon, the repercussions of their musical revolution continued, and still do, to take Beatle history beyond its natural conclusion.

The very first annual Beatles Appreciation Convention occurred in Boston, Massachusetts, over a weekend in July 1974. It entailed a giant auction and flea market of Beatle rarities, and six continuous hours of rare films about The Beatles were screened.

That same year a new play about The Beatles, *John, Paul, George, Ringo . . . and Bert*, opened in London to rave reviews and enthusiastic audiences. At about the same time the musical *Sgt Pepper's Lonely Hearts Club Band On The Road* opened in America, and the following year Robert Stigwood, who had produced *Jesus Christ Superstar*, began preparing a film version of *Sgt Pepper's Lonely Hearts Club Band* featuring The Bee Gees as the band of the title.

The first British Beatle convention was held in Norwich in August 1975 at which a large selection of Beatle *memorabilia* was sold. By the mid-Sixties an abundance of Beatle merchandise had sprung up – t-shirts, dishes, dolls, hats, stockings and of course the wigs – the list is endless. Yet one of the very early pioneers of Beatle merchandise told me that at the beginning the only kind of merchandise any fan could get was big posters which were sold outside venues for concerts. In those days there always used to be more fans outside than in.

I was told that the people who sold outside concerts then used to make a very good living as there was no competition from the official Beatles promoters. It was only when the promoters saw what a good living the outside sellers were making that they decided to cash in and sell official merchandise. Before then, there was none.

Eventually, competition became so great between the original, outside merchandisers and the official ones that the promoters began calling in the police to have the 'bootleggers' moved on. It seems a shame to me that the people who started the whole business of selling merchandise at concerts should have been pushed into the background.

The old Beatles fan magazine that had enjoyed a successful publishing run in the Sixties was resurrected in August 1976, helping to keep the spirit of Beatlemania alive.

There was, however, a tragic event that occurred the same year. Mal Evans, The Beatles' roadie and close friend, was shot to death by American police in Los Angeles. It happened at the home of Mal's girlfriend, Frances Hughes, who called the police saying that Mal was distraught and had taken her little girl into a bedroom, armed with a shotgun. When Mal refused to surrender the rifle, the police opened fire and shot him six times.

I have clear memories of Mal Evans as a cheerful, personable fellow, but in recent months he had become suicidal. At the time of his death he had been writing a book about his association with The Beatles. I recall some time back, when I began working on my book, talking to Mal about it and him telling me that he was going to write his own. I'm sure he would have had quite a story to tell.

In 1977 another musical opened in America – *Beatlemania*. It was comprised of 49 Beatle songs, using all the original recordings which the actors involved mimed to. Such shows and films may not have been anywhere near as satisfying as the real thing, but it was all we had to remind us of better days, and shows such as *Beatlemania* were as close as anyone could get then to watching a real Beatles concert.

In 1978 the movie *I Want To Hold Your Hand* came out, retelling the story of the day The Beatles appeared on the Ed

Sullivan TV show. Actual TV footage from that show, clever-
ly mixed with long shots and clever angles of four Beatle
lookalikes whom you never quite see, helped to create an
impression of the real Beatles.

Better still, the following year a television feature film was
produced called *Birth Of The Beatles*, featuring four actors
who bore uncanny resemblances to the real Fab Four and who
each gave accurate and convincing performances.

But what every fan really hoped for was to see the real
Beatles do their own thing together again. All that was put to
a definite end when John died.

The death of Lennon seemed to bring the other three closer
together, and when Ringo married Barbara Bach in 1981,
both George and Paul were at the wedding.

It was suddenly very much like the old days when, during
the wedding reception, an impromptu jam session ensued
between Paul on piano, George on guitar and Ringo on drums
in a rousing rendition of *I Saw Her Standing There*.

Now, if only they would do that sort of thing in public!

Beatle history was still being made, even in 1981. The
Liverpool Council finally gave in to pressure to have four new
streets named after The Beatles. They were John Lennon
Drive, Paul McCartney Way, George Harrison Close and
Ringo Starr Drive. The council was aware that the street signs
of Penny Lane and Abbey Road in London had been removed by ardent fans, so Liverpool's four new street signs
were all placed well out of arm's reach.

Well, it still goes on. Beatle conventions continue to take
place all over the world every year and promoters and producers still continue to try and get the surviving members of
the group to perform publicly. Who knows, maybe one day
they will. One thing is for sure, their fan following remains as
loyal as ever. In 1983 they flocked from all around the globe to
a special Beatles 'Sound On Sight' show which was held for a
week at the EMI studios in Abbey Road. Beatles music and
yet more rare film was shown.

Today such exhibitions, conventions and eagerly awaited
records by the individual Beatles are probably all we can
expect. Certainly nobody goes Beatlewatching any more, at
least not to the extent I and my friends did so long ago. It

would be impossible to do that now anyway because since John's murder, security around the Beatles has tightened.

George has said, 'All of us Beatles got a bit shirty about strangers barging up to us. You can't be sure if they wanted to shoot you or not. After what happened to John, I don't like to be in the flashlight.'

Yesterday will never return. Perhaps that's why we try so hard to snatch a little of what we all had yesterday, although so often it's in vain because, like The Beatles, like the fans even (we all grow older), nothing stays the same. Even when fans make pilgrimages in their thousands to Metthew Street in Liverpool where the famous Cavern Club played host to The Beatles at the very onset of their career, they see little to remind them of the Beatles, or show them what it was all like.

That's because the original Cavern was pulled down to make way for a branch of the local underground railway. Another 'Cavern' was built across the road, but it never rivalled the original and wasn't even called the Cavern but 'Eric's'.

A peculiar footnote to all this is that there is a strange metal statue which graces the wall of Eric's. It's a tribute by sculptor Arthur Dooley to The Beatles. Underneath there is a plaque which reads, 'Four lads who shook the world.'

The statue represents a Madonna holding three babies in her arms. A fourth baby is flying away, blowing a trumpet. The Madonna symbolizes Merseyside, the mother of the four boys. The escaping cherub represents Paul because, in the opinion of Dooley, The Beatles split up because Paul left.

Well, everyone has their opinions as to why The Beatles broke up. You know my opinions now. After all, I did see it all happening – as much as any fan could – and I'm glad that I did. They were the best years – and perhaps occasionally the worst – of my life.

Bibliography

The Beatles, Hunter Davies, McGraw-Hill, 1968

A Day In The Life, compiled by Tom Schultheiss, Omnibus Press, 1980

The Beatles A to Z, compiled by Goldie Friede, Robin Titone and Sue Weiner, Eyre Methuen Ltd, 1981

The Beatles Concerted Efforts, compiled by Jan Van de Bunt and friends, Beatles Unlimited, 1979

26 Days That Rocked The World, O'Brien, 1978

The Beatles Book, publisher and editor Johnny Dean

Record Mirror, Spotlight Publications Ltd

Sounds, Spotlight Publications Ltd

Melody Maker, IPC Magazines Ltd

New Musical Express, IPC Magazines Ltd

Various British daily papers

The Beatles – 25 Years in the life, Mark Lewisohn, 1987